Enterprise Evolution, Survival and the *Businesstype*

The strategic journey taken by firms starts with entrepreneurial inception and can go all the way through adaptation to sustainable enterprise, exit, or failure. This book charts how new ventures grow through co-evolution and adaptation to get past the initial problems of being new, connecting theories of strategic management and entrepreneurship.

Conceptually, the author paints an integrated picture of the challenges arising from the enterprise life cycle. Based on research, this book is also accessible to practitioners and students, in that it provides practice-oriented takeaways about how enterprises can evolve and thrive in turbulent times.

Together with executives, entrepreneurs, and policymakers, this book is intended for scholars and postgraduate students, interested in understanding strategic management and entrepreneurship from an evolutionary perspective.

Gianpaolo Abatecola is Full Professor of Management at the University of Rome Tor Vergata, Italy.

Routledge Focus on Business and Management

The fields of business and management have grown exponentially as areas of research and education. This growth presents challenges for readers trying to keep up with the latest important insights. *Routledge Focus on Business and Management* presents small books on big topics and how they intersect with the world of business research.

Individually, each title in the series provides coverage of a key academic topic, while collectively, the series forms a comprehensive collection across the business disciplines.

Digital Transformation of Performing Arts
Trends in the Classical Music Industry
Salvino A. Salvaggio

Globalization and Entrepreneurship
Cases from China, Japan, and Bangladesh
Mirjana Radović-Marković, Yao Ouyang, and Md. Shajahan Kabir

Comparative Dynamics in the Comics Industry
Contrasting Cultures in France, Belgium, and the Netherlands
Rudi de Vries

Reimagining Organizational Change
Richard J. Badham and Brenda M. Santiago

Nostalgic Branding in the Toy Industry
Kamil Lubiński and Magdalena Grębosz-Krawczyk

Enterprise Evolution, Survival and the *Businesstype*
From Research to Practice
Gianpaolo Abatecola

For more information about this series, please visit: www.routledge.com/Routledge-Focus-on-Business-and-Management/book-series/FBM

Enterprise Evolution, Survival and the *Businesstype*

From Research to Practice

Gianpaolo Abatecola

Routledge
Taylor & Francis Group
LONDON AND NEW YORK

First published 2025
by Routledge
4 Park Square, Milton Park, Abingdon, Oxon OX14 4RN

and by Routledge
605 Third Avenue, New York, NY 10158

Routledge is an imprint of the Taylor & Francis Group, an informa business

British Library Cataloguing-in-Publication Data
A catalogue record for this book is available from the British Library

ISBN: 9781032535715 (hbk)
ISBN: 9781032535739 (pbk)
ISBN: 9781003412663 (ebk)

DOI: 10.4324/9781003412663

Typeset in Times New Roman
by codeMantra

To my wife, Michela and to my son, Roberto Mattia
My forces of evolution and survival

To my mother, Nives and to my father, Franco
My forces of ancestry and businesstype

Contents

Illustrations

Figures

Tables

Boxes

Preface

"Daddy, do you know Raichu?". "No, Roby, I do not". "Daddy, Raichu represents the *evolution* of Pikachu!".

Focused on the evolution of Pikachu, which is the main character of the famous Pokémon anime series, for much time this question/answer session with my child has constituted, especially recently, a daily component of my family life. Indeed, my daily work life is not much different; how enterprises can survive in the mid of disruption, and how their decisions can affect their evolution, are questions that have always driven my research curiosity as a management scholar and educator. I am passionate about investigating these topics; it also guides how I teach, provide students with professional development, foster academia-industry connections, and perform institutional service.

On this premise, where does this book project come from? In general, I am part of an international community of management scholars who use to make comparisons with biology, and also use insights from psychology, to analyse key business phenomena, such as firm and industry competition, new ventures' early survival or death, and corporate crises or turnaround processes. In particular, the *origin* of this book dates back to many years ago. I presented a literature review paper about organizational adaptation and survival in our evolutionary track (to date in the Research Methods and Research Practice Strategic Interest Group) at the Annual Conference of the European Academy of Management in Rotterdam. Among the valuable feedback received, one main recurring suggestion was that the paper's contents could have appeared too many for a single journal article, while, if properly developed, they could have found a more *fitting* home in a book. In the same year, a similar feedback is what I received when presenting the paper at the Annual Meeting of the Academy of Management in Boston (Organization and Management Theory Division). This book is thus (at least) a demonstration that I never forgot those feedbacks!

The above introduced, this book aims to provide its readers with a review of different but intertwined key themes regarding enterprise evolution as a research area in the strategic management domain. In particular, Chapter 1 focuses on what forces, in principle, substantially drive the evolution of enterprises and, thus, whether it should be considered externally pulled (i.e., primarily shaped by the environment) or internally pushed (i.e., primarily shaped by firms themselves). Accordingly, Chapter 2 concentrates on the specific survival problems of new-born enterprises, while Chapter 3 deals, more in general, with enterprise survival or failure across later stages of the life cycle. Finally, Chapter 4 presents avenues for research and practice for each of these themes.

Also given the amount of theories and constructs analysed in its chapters, this book has no ambition of resulting exhaustive in terms of literature discussed. At the same time, however, this book can provide a contribution which is both conceptual and methodological. From a conceptual point of view, it can perhaps offer a more integrated picture about challenges regarding the enterprise life cycle which are often observed through a more single-focused lens. From a methodological point of view, although research-based, this book is written in a way that intends to speak not only to scholars of strategic management (and, from more than one aspect, of entrepreneurship as well) but also to practitioners and students. In fact, the concepts explained are often preceded or followed by real-world examples from the practice of business. In some cases, these concepts are also associated with a sort of some "Easter eggs" from my classroom experience over time. Relatedly, Chapter 4 precisely ends with some "how to" practice-oriented takeaways about how enterprises can evolve and thrive in our turbulent times.

Intended for board members, managers, entrepreneurs, and policymakers, these takeaways directly draw on my impact blog *The Businesstype*. Over the years, I have ideally thought of the term "Businesstype" to stimulate an intellectual comparison with the genotype and phenotype in natural sciences. In line with the underlying spirit of this book, this is why I have also chosen this term as a (hopefully) representative part of its title. In this regard, I am grateful to Terry Clague from Routledge for having supported this book project in general, and also this idea in particular.

Gianpaolo Abatecola, PhD
Full Professor of Management
Tor Vergata University of Rome
December 3, 2024

1 Enterprise evolution as a research field

1.1 Introduction

We could argue that, over time, the core focus of those scholars interested in understanding how enterprises *evolve* has been, in principle, the theoretical and empirical study of drivers, dynamics, and consequences regarding the competitive (*lato sensu*) relationship between enterprises and their environment. The kinds of enterprise considered have been many, varying both in terms of dimension and age. Actualizing the field to the current business arena, examples of investigated dimension would range, for instance, from small/medium-sized enterprises, such as many family firms all around the world, to big corporations, such as Amazon; in parallel, examples of age would range from start-ups, such as the promising Tesla in the early 2000s, to mature, such as General Motors, and even declining firms, such as the Chinese real estate giant Evergrande in 2022. At the same time, the kinds of environmental objects of attention have also been various, ranging from the internal context, such as a specific level within the governance-management-operations organizational hierarchy, to the external setting, such as a particular industry (e.g., car automakers) or macro-economic (e.g., region, country, or continent-based) scenario.

On this premise, this chapter seeks to discuss some initial borders which, both from a conceptual and methodological point of view, might result useful to characterize "enterprise evolution" as a per se research field in the strategic management domain. In this regard, it seems sensible to start with considering that, when applied to enterprises, the concept of evolution has been generally referred to as a firm's change, over time, which is a consequence, or also a determinant, of successful survival processes. On the one hand, let us consider this change as a determinant by recalling the mergers and acquisitions often occurring, for example in the car industry, to improve competitiveness; in January 2021, the well-known Fiat Chrysler Automobiles and Peugeot SA groups gave birth to the current Stellantis. On the other hand, and remaining in the same industry, let us also consider this change as a consequence by considering that, at the beginning of this century, the Italian Fiat heavily recentralized its business portfolio into the core (i.e., car production) to survive a crisis.

DOI: 10.4324/9781003412663-1

Drawing on the examples above, from the beginning it seems evident that, assuming a traditional strategic management perspective, the field of enterprise evolution studies competition in general and phenomena associated with Michael Porter's competitive advantage (1985) in particular. At the same time, however, and as the term "evolution" can easily evoke, from the beginning it seems also evident that, as a key distinctive feature, the development of this research area has been largely inspired by comparisons with how competition in general, and evolution in particular, occur in natural sciences (e.g., Cafferata, 2016; Burgelman et al., 2023). In other words, as this chapter explains, enterprise evolution (as a field) owes much to Charles Darwin's *The Origin of Species* (1859), and, over time, also to the work of other eminent scholars, such as Gregor Mendel (Levinthal, 2021), in biology-related fields.

The attempt to discuss the perimeter of enterprise evolution as a per se research area in the strategic management domain is, undoubtedly, challenging (Durand, 2006). In fact, the number of schools of thought (or of scholars individually) that have explained competition through using comparisons, at different degrees of similarity, with natural sciences, has been massive over time. For example, in the pioneering words of Lawrence Hrebiniak and William Joyce, "the term 'organizational adaptation' has been employed in a number of ways, ranging simply from change, including both proactive and reactive behaviour, to a more specific denotation of reaction to environmental forces or demands" (1985: 387). This introduction outlines the structure of this chapter as follows. First, this chapter considers what main theories have generally derived their conceptual underpinnings from the evolutionary process in natural sciences. Second, this chapter synthesizes a long-standing dichotomy between many of these theories, which has been the debate around what, between "environmental determinism" (i.e., *the environment always counts more than firms*) and "strategic voluntarism" (i.e., *firms always count more than the environment*), mainly determines the adaptation and evolution of enterprises. Third, this chapter explains how those approaches known as "dialectical" have gradually reduced this dichotomy. Fourth, this chapter ends with a focus on the "co-evolutionary" perspective. Developed, since the late 1990s, on the legacy of the dialectical approaches, to date co-evolution has seemingly reached wide consensus, in the strategic management domain, when one seeks to analyse how competition works. Summary and takeaways for scholars, practitioners, and students conclude this chapter.

1.2 Enterprises evolve. How?

In the early 2000s, I was a university student approaching to choose the topic of the final dissertation thesis, needed to be written for graduating. In those years, one case from the business world that soon gained massive media attention (and caught my attention too) was that of the American Enron corporation. Founded in 1985 through the merger of Houston Natural Gas (Texas) and InterNorth (Nebraska), at the beginning Enron was a traditional hard asset public utility, active in natural gas distribution. Very soon, however, the company *evolved* into a sort of global financial conglomerate, active in the trading of energy-related commodities (e.g., gas, electricity, water, and steel). This case is still sadly famous. In 2000, Fortune Business magazine named Enron "The Most Innovative Company in America" for the fifth continuous year and ranked it at number 7 in its specific Fortune 500 ranking. In December 2001, however, Enron declared bankruptcy after a series of judicial inquiries revealed it had committed financial fraud.

From the example above, it seems evident that, in principle, the term "evolution" reflects a general idea of change *also* when enterprises are concerned. "*Also*" is here written in italics because it seems contemporaneously evident that this generic idea of evolution, as a change, in the business world does not look much different from the idea of evolution, as a change, in the natural world. In the former, Enron evolved from a traditional gas distributor to a global financial intermediary. In the latter, the little Guanlong Wucaii mostly located in China evolved into the huge Tyrannosaurus Rex mostly located in the Americas (Osborn, 1905). In this regard, explaining how evolution happens in the natural world is certainly beyond the scope of this book in general, and of this chapter in particular. However, standing on the shoulders of Darwin, we might consider that the following synthesis could still prove somewhat useful: when species of living beings are under observation, evolution can be substantially considered a continuous, structural change of these species over time. The observable degree of this change varies according to the time span through which it is analysed. The change appears weak in the short term, while it appears massive in the long term. In this regard, for example, we might again think that the Guanlong Wucaii was about 3-meters long (for about 75 kilos), while, after several geological eras, the biggest Tyrannosaurus Rex had become more than 10-meters long (for about 6 tons). If we simplify the core tenets of the "modern evolutionary synthesis" (Huxley, 1942), also labelled as "standard evolutionary theory" to date (Laland et al., 2014), in the natural world evolution substantially happens because:

i "natural selection" determines what species survive and what species do not, with survival determined by the presence of *variations* between and among species. Variations can be intended here as differences in the presence of those organic features/behaviours necessary to "fit" the environment (for example, there is only one leaf on a tree, and two giraffes with two differently long necks; the giraffe with the longest neck can reach the leaf, and survives because can feed itself, while the giraffe with the smallest neck perishes because cannot);

ii through reproduction, those species surviving natural selection transmit their parental *genetic code* to the offsprings (for example, successors resemble their ancestors);
iii there is a *random* component in how the genetic code (sub ii) is transmitted (for example, successors are similar, but never perfectly equal to their ancestors).

The above introduced, and as far as the world of economics and business is concerned, especially from the second half of the past century various theories of *evolutionary* change have been advanced (e.g., Gowdy et al., 2013; Aldrich et al., 2020). As a conceptual start, in 1965 Donald Campbell published his *Variation and Selective Retention in Socio-cultural Evolution*. The core tenet of this landmark piece of research is that, also in social sciences, phenomena of long-term change can be understood through applying the biological process of *variation* (of the "genotype"), *selection* (of the associated "phenotype"), and *retention* (of the underlying "genotype").

On this basis, if, for example, we consider macro perspectives, in 1977, Michael Hannan and John Freeman develop "population ecology" to explain the long-term change, in terms of founding, survival, or failure, of organizational *populations* and *communities* (with populations to be intended as groups of organizations featured by the same characteristics, and communities to be conceived as the networks of relationships within and between these populations). Relatedly, at the micro level, the famous book *An Evolutionary Theory of Economic Change*, written in 1982 by Richard Nelson and Sidney Winter, introduces the analogy, in terms of the role played for survival purposes, between genes in natural sciences and *routines* in organizations (e.g., Becker, 2004). Subsequently, and with an even wider spectrum of analysis (e.g., Stoelhorst, 2008), Generalized Darwinism has argued that, if certain degrees of abstraction are assumed, the main mechanisms surrounding Darwin's evolutionary theory can be also used to appropriately explain the evolution of entire socio-economic systems (Hodgson and Knudsen, 2010). In this regard, "replicator" and "interactor" have been the two concepts mostly used as substitutes of genotypes and phenotypes, respectively (Breslin, 2011). Quoting David Hull (1988: 488), a replicator is something of which copies are made, while an interactor is "an entity that directly interacts as a cohesive whole with its environment in such a way that this interaction causes replication to be differential".[1] To explain cultural evolution, for example, Richard Dawkins' (1976) concept of "memes" has been, since its introduction, largely used as the replicator (e.g., Schlaile, 2021; Gill and Price, 2022).

With the above explained, in this initial overview other significant perspectives also seemingly merit attention because of their specific approaches used. In particular, we might argue that, although these perspectives have not necessarily stemmed from the Darwinian assumptions to explain evolution in the business world, they have still heavily drawn from natural sciences (e.g., Johansson and Kask, 2013; Abatecola, 2014). In some perspectives, for example, the evolution of enterprises in general, and of their life cycle in particular, has been conceived, from various aspects, as similar to that of living beings. Similarities have included, among others, the stages of birth/introduction, growth, maturity, and decline/death, supposed as sequential and predictable. Some other perspectives, however, have discussed organizational life cycles also drawing on the fascinating theory of "punctuated equilibrium" elaborated in palaeontology (Eldredge and Gould, 1972). This theory, in substance, contrasts Darwin's idea that, although gradual, evolution is a continuous process. In particular, as observed by Niles Eldredge and Stephen Jay Gould, during most of their existence a number of fossils do not change at all. When these fossils change, however, their evolution is sudden (i.e., punctuated), fast, and radical. In strategic management and entrepreneurship, punctuated equilibrium has been found to be a reliable instrument to study, both *ex ante* and *ex post*, the evolutionary dynamics of various industries (e.g., Phelps et al., 2007), such as that of the minicomputer producers in the US (Romanelli and Tushman, 1994).

To conclude, it could also appear worth noticing here that, with regard to the perspectives already commented on, population ecology has been, for example, formally presented as Darwinian, but, over time, has been conceptually associated also with non-Darwinian surroundings (e.g., Reydon and Scholz, 2009). In contrast, while Nelson and Winter have, at least from some aspects, presented their theoretical approach as Lamarckian, over time scholars have, more than once, also highlighted its Darwinian foundations (Grandinetti, 2018).

1.3 Enterprises adapt. How?

From some aspects, we are still all recovering from the disruptions recently brought by COVID-19 and the business world does not seemingly constitute an exception. The pandemic has been a tremendous, unexpected shock worldwide. Many firms were not able to survive this shock and those which resulted successful were those able to *adapt* their capabilities to the sudden, radical change brought in their value chain by this shock (e.g., Foss, 2021). For instance, many restaurants were forced to close because of the physiological impossibility to maintain their profitability through their traditional food consumption experience (for several months, during the lockdown, clients had to remain home). Relatedly, as we have seen, those restaurants which were able to maintain a minimum viable level of profitability were those resulting flexible to quickly convert their traditional food and beverage selling into pick-up and home delivery services. In contrast, as we have also seen, some industries did not require particular forms of reaction to the environmental change brought by COVID-19. For example, Amazon *adapted* and continued to remain highly competitive, but the most vivid features characterizing its business model did not seemingly witness particular transformations.

Drawing on the examples above, our attempt to classify strategic management perspectives, paradigms and schools of thought in the enterprise evolution research field continues. The main rationale used in the previous section, i.e., comparisons with natural sciences, remains unaltered. At this stage, however, we no longer focus on the core principles, synthesized in the previous pages, of any (standard) evolutionary process, but on the main determinant of this process, which, as also introduced above, is the term "adaptation". In natural sciences, this term has generally referred to the relationship between organisms and their natural environment and, more specifically, it has substantiated the process in which the former searches for the most appropriate "fit" into the latter (e.g., Lewontin, 1978). Those organisms which are not able to adapt are *selected out* by the environment. On the contrary, those organisms able to adapt are *selected in* and evolve through reproduction. Standard evolutionary theory considers adaptation, from more than one aspect, as a process featured by a relevant *deterministic* component. This means that, in this process, the environment substantially expresses a primacy in determining what organisms are selected in and what organisms are selected out.

On this basis, while not formally using the core evolutionary mechanisms (i.e., variation, selection, and retention) in their models, a number of strategic management perspectives have instead referred to adaptation, stressing its deterministic view. For instance, one famous portrait of this view has been expressed by "contingency" theory (*it all depends*) in the 1960s. In principle, this theory has advanced that no *one best way* to manage enterprises is possible and that the competitive environment primarily determines what kinds of organizational structure firms need to use to be (or remain) profitable over time. More specifically, for example, the famous analysis by Paul Lawrence and Jay Lorsch (1967) reveals that environmental dynamism increases the need to adopt internally differentiated organizational structures. The increase of internal differentiation, in turn, raises the need for integration, with the degree for this need being, in principle, case-specific. Relatedly, it has been argued that contingency theory presents many deterministic arguments similar to those, subsequently, representing the core of "neo-institutional" theory (Di Maggio and Powell, 1983). However, while the former theory has basically explained that the environment determines *why* organizational structures vary, the latter theory has explained that the environment can also determine *why* firms within the same industry can have the same core characteristics (i.e., "isomorphism"). In the view of neo-institutionalism, any specific kind of environment generates intra-industry homogeneity, because it forces all its firms to embrace the same forms of strategic and organizational adaptation to its markets standards, social principles, and customers' attitudes.

The above explained, we should consider that the deterministic view of adaptation is not the only view developed in strategic management. Advancing orientations towards "voluntarism", a number of schools of thought have, in contrast, also emerged and they are far from being potentially considered deterministic to date. Although at different degrees of intensity, voluntarism substantially highlights the role of the firms' strategic intentionality and free will in their adaptive relationship with the environment (e.g., Malerba and Lee, 2017; McCarthy et al., 2017). In this regard, one of the most pioneering expressions of voluntarism has been that introduced by John Child with his "strategic choice" theory in the 1970s. In contrast to the contingency perspectives developed in the 1960s, Child proposes strategic choice as "the process whereby power-holders within organizations decide upon course of strategic action […] Strategic choice extends to the environment within which the pressure of economic constraints has to be evaluated and to the design of the organization's structure itself" (1972: 2). Child, in substance, puts forward that, when planning strategies, the firm's top decision-makers can be always proactive in terms of time, nature, and methods of the decisions to be taken. In other terms, he argues that, as far as determinism and voluntarism are concerned, it is the latter, rather than the former, which mostly shapes the strategic decision-making (and associated performance) of enterprises. Relatedly, the most famous portrait of voluntarism is, to date, probably the "upper echelons" theory. Drawing upon Herbert Simon's "bounded rationality" (1947), and Richard Cyert and James March's "behavioural theory of the firm" (1963), in their theory Donald Hambrick and Phyllis Mason (1984) argue that behavioural determinants in general, and the cognitive bases of the firm's top dominant coalition, are the most significant driver of Child's strategic choice. According to Hambrick and Mason, *organizations become reflections of their top executives*. In their framework, the "socio-demographic features" (e.g., age, education, functional tracks, socio-economic roots, tenure) of the firm's dominant coalition are key factors. Over time, research on upper echelons has become massively popular worldwide, with the flourishing of analyses regarding the relationship between the socio-demographic features (and, later, also personality traits) of dominant coalitions and a number of different strategic outcomes (e.g., M&As, partnerships, financialization, and turnarounds).

At least since the second half of the past century, much of the scholarly debate around how enterprises adapt (and then evolve) can be explained as the debate around the dichotomy between determinism and voluntarism in shaping their adaptation (Astley and Van de Ven, 1983). How can this dichotomy be synthesized? We could argue that, on the one hand, determinism has mostly conceived organizational adaptation as a process in which, substantially, enterprises can *only* react to environmental expectations and changes. The environment, as a whole, appears as a sum of totally rational agents, with its macro-economic dynamics primarily determining the strategic decision-making of these agents. Voluntarism, on the other hand, has pushed towards the possibility of *also* strongly proactive strategic decision-making by the agents. Dependent on their bounded rationality and subjectivity, according to voluntarists, these agents are those which, from the internal, chiefly drive the adaptation process. In this regard, for example, about 20 years after having developed his strategic choice theory, Child again comments on the determinism/voluntarism dichotomy, by arguing that "the deterministic view was inadequate because of its failure to give due attention to the agency of choice by whoever have the power to direct the organization" (1997: 45).

At this point, it seems thus also clear that, by prioritizing strategic intentionality, and thus by assuming that enterprises can also result independent of their competitive context, voluntarists have consistently departed from the perspective of organizational adaptation and evolution as purely deterministic. At the same time, placing also voluntarism *within* the borders of the enterprise evolution research field can provide, we believe, both scholars and practitioners with a more updated and complete overview of the field (e.g., Abatecola, 2012; Sarta et al., 2021). Relatedly, we could conclude by asking how the determinism/voluntarism dichotomy has evolved. On this side, we could state that, over time, this dichotomy has gradually found a convergence and, to date, it appears much less strong than it appeared in the past century. The main reason why the dichotomy has been reduced can be primarily found in the introduction and, subsequently, the gradual development of conceptual models (and associated empirical analyses), which have investigated on the adaptation process through adopting more middle-ground perspectives. Categorized as "dialectical" (Van de Ven and Poole, 1995), these perspectives have put forward the assumption that, when studying the determinants of adaptation, environmental determinism and strategic voluntarism have necessarily to be jointly (and cannot be separately) considered.

Drawing on these perspectives, some models have (even more specifically) advanced that, to be fully understood, the study of adaptation needs to be dynamic in nature. In particular, when considering the overall life cycle of most of the enterprises, the influence relationship between firms (i.e., voluntarism) and their competitive environment (i.e., determinism) changes. When this influence relationship changes, the resulting effect, in terms of adaptation, also varies. In sum, as these models have maintained, a dynamic approach to adaptation allows us to capture what a static approach physiologically cannot. In this regard, we could even go back to the pioneering words of Edith Penrose (1959: 5): "As management tries to make the best use of resources available, a truly dynamic interacting process occurs which encourages continuous growth but limits the rate of growth".

1.4 Adaptation is dialectical. Why?

In business schools, positive examples of superstar entrepreneurs and CEOs, such as Elon Musk, Giorgio Armani, Jeff Bezos, Richard Branson, or Jack Ma, are often those which we use to inspire our students when starting our management classes at undergraduate, graduate, and, especially, executive level. Think about Elon Musk. With great charisma, he has literally convinced various stakeholders – customers, partners, and employees – to dream with him that life on another planet is possible. Whenever I present start-ups and the story of SpaceX to students, I can see how the company's value proposition resonates with them. Their engagement level increases, frequently leading to robust conversations. Mr. Musk's vision has cascaded from offices in California to classrooms all around the world!

The examples above can also represent a (hopefully) useful introduction to the main underpinnings surrounding the dialectical approach to the study of the relationship between enterprises and their environment. In this regard, dialectical thinking in management and organization theory certainly owes many of its origins to the pioneering thought of Karl Weick in the late 1960s. In its inspiring book *The Social Psychology of Organizing* (1969), Weick introduces the concept of "sense-making" to understand reality. According to Weick, reality is not objective but is something which is "enacted" (i.e., given sense to) by humans. This process of enactment is driven by the combined mix between the individuals' background, experience, and cognitive mechanisms. Retrospectively influencing their life conduct, the enacted reality in turn activates a *circular* relationship with individuals. Subsequently, Kenneth Benson (1977) more specifically advances the need to adopt dialectical thinking in the study of organizational adaptation. In contrast to the extant dichotomy between voluntarism and determinism of that period, Benson's ideas were ground-breaking because contend that the proper unit of analysis should be the *process of interaction*, rather than the individual behaviour of the entities (i.e., enterprises on the one hand and the environment on the other) interacting. In particular, Benson's view of adaptation, as the result of this process of interaction, reflects the famous, historical concept of "synthesis" in Friedrich Hegel's *Phänomenologie des Geistes* (1807); in turn, firms and environments reflect Hegel's concepts of "thesis" and "antithesis", respectively.

On this premise, one of the first attempts, in the 1980s, to reconcile the determinism/voluntarism dichotomy through the dialectical approach is that by Jay Bourgeois (1984). Introducing the terms "domain definition" and "domain navigation", first Bourgeois supports the idea that voluntarism (i.e., domain definition) and determinism (i.e., domain navigation) are both always present. Defining a domain means *enacting* the environment and planning what performance may want to be achieved within it. In parallel, navigating a domain means behaving within this environment, which now serves as the main selector of appropriate and inappropriate behaviours. Second, and relatedly, Bourgeois admits the

> "possibility of reciprocal causation among external (environmental or contextual) factors, strategic decisions, and internal (structural, power and resources distribution) factors. So, though environmental and internal forces

> act as constraints, strategy making often selects and later modifies the sets of constraints. Dialectical thinking will be required to countenance this state of affairs, which might be described as an interactive tension between the inertia of environmental and internal forces and the kinetics of strategic choice".
>
> (pp. 592–593)

In parallel, a breakthrough, still thought-provoking theoretical framework is elaborated by Hrebiniak and Joyce (1985), who posit that

> "the interdependence and interactions between strategic choice and environmental determinism define adaptation; each is insufficient and both are necessary to a satisfactory explication of organizational adaptation. Adaptation is a dynamic process that is the result of the relative strength and type of power or dependency between organization and the environment ... Both strategic choice and environmental determinism provide trusts for change; each is both a cause and consequence of the other in the adaptation process ... To understand this dynamic change phenomenon, it is necessary to think in circles, to investigate the reciprocity of relationships between organization and environment, and to study the mutual causation that obtains".
>
> (pp. 346–347)

In this vein, Hrebiniak and Joyce formalize an "adaptation matrix", composed of four different quadrants: Quadrant I (high determinism, low strategic choice); Quadrant II (high determinism, high strategic choice); Quadrant III (low determinism, high strategic choice); Quadrant IV (low determinism, low strategic choice). As they argue, it appears clear that, (at least) from a *static* point of view, different configurations of organizational competitive positioning are possible, with these configurations depending on the different, possible combinations of determinism and choice. At the same time, they also argue, a related, promising interpretative lens can benefit, in the future, from integrating their approach with a *dynamic* perspective. This perspective, in particular, can focus on studying how these configurations can change, over time, when the intensity of determinism and/or choice varies.

Empirical tests of Hrebiniak and Joyce's framework soon followed, with some among the most well-known conducted through qualitative case study methodologies. Andrew Pettigrew (1987), for example, studies the determinants of the strategic change occurring at the British industrial company ICI (Imperial Chemical Industries) between 1960 and 1984, a change which he groups into three main periods (1960–1964, 1970–1972, and 1980–1986). On the one hand, Pettigrew observes that the high degree of change in all these periods is often associated with world economic recessions, which put pressures on ICI performance. In other terms, ICI was induced to radical changes especially when it faced performance decline. However, as Pettigrew also observes:

> "A critical facet of these change periods was not only the perception and reality of business pressure, but also the active strategies by managers to construct a climate for change around the performance difficulties. Mobilizing the outer content in order to provide the legitimacy and justification for change was a critical part of the political learning process of change. The revolutionary periods of change were also connected with changes in leadership and power at ICI".
>
> (pp. 664–665)

In sum, a substantive analytical support to the Hrebniak and Joyce's continuity hypothesis between determinism and voluntarism.

Another case study leading to aligned findings is that by Robert Burgelman (1991) on the strategic decision-making process implemented by the leading semiconductor INTEL in the period 1985–1989. Burgelman notes the concurring presence of both an "induced" and "autonomous" process. While the former process reflects (internal) environmental determinism, the latter can be easily associated with voluntarism. In this regard: "The induced process concerns initiatives that are within the scope of the organization's current strategy and build on existing organizational learning; the autonomous process concerns initiatives that emerge outside of it and provide the potential for new organizational learning" (p. 241). By testing Hrebiniak and Joyce's framework through (for the first time) a quantitative research design, Michael Lawless and Linda Finch's analysis (1989) results, instead, methodologically different from the case studies conducted by Pettigrew and Burgelman. To conduct their study, Lawless and Finch use Gregory Dess and Donald Beard's (1984) construct of environmental dimensions (i.e., "munificence", "complexity", and "dynamism"), together with their categorization of 52 four-digit Standard Industrial Classification industries. In parallel, they group a sample of 146 firms into strategic clusters drawing on Danny Miller's (1986) four business-level strategy types (i.e., "differentiation", "cost leadership", "focus", and "asset parsimony"). In this case, their resulting taxonomy provides only partial support to Hrebiniak and Joyce's framework.

All the above explained, some subsequent perspectives about organizational adaptation also try to advance the ideas of Hrebiniak and Joyce. For example, in Richard Whittington's "realist" perspective (1988), human agency is limited by a pre-existing structure.[2] However, Whittington argues, this "structure is not atomized, as in action determinism; nor does it crush human agency, as in environmental determinism; nor finally is it subordinate, as interpretative voluntarists assume" (p. 528). Relatedly, considering organizational adaptation as *dynamic* has represented one main conceptual foundation of the approach developed by Roberto Cafferata over time (e.g., 2022). In his dialectical view of the organization/environment relationship, Cafferata considers any firm's life cycle potentially divided into two macro phases sequentially, but not necessarily always, occurring. Featured by a strongly deterministic component, the first phase resembles *natural selection* and lasts, on average, the first three to four years; in this phase, start-ups present, on average, high mortality rates and are mostly confined to survival scopes (i.e., to make a parallelism with genetics [Lewontin, 1983], firms are "object" of the evolutionary process). Named "competitive selection", the second phase instead regards all those (once start-ups) firms which have survived natural selection. In this case, Cafferata argues, firms can activate forms of environmental control, which can even enable them to become market leaders and game changers (i.e., again with Richard Lewontin, firms become "subject" of the evolutionary process). Overall, Cafferata thus puts forward two possible kinds of adaptation paths during any firm's life cycle and, in parallel, several "grey" areas (i.e., potential transitory stages within these paths). The former path is "virtuous" and substantiates a positive evolutionary process (e.g., as the result of a successful growth strategy); "contradictory", the latter instead features a negative evolutionary process, which can even end with the firm's failure.

1.5 Enterprises co-evolve. How?

With a population of circa 45,000, my hometown of Frosinone constitutes one of the five Province County Seats of the Lazio Region in Italy. The Frosinone Football Club plays its home matches in the Benito Stirpe PSC Arena Football Stadium. Inaugurated at the end of September 2017, the stadium is formally dedicated to the memory of Cavalier Benito Stirpe, a magnificent entrepreneur and a memorable patron of the club. Also thanks to its UK-inspired, modern and comfortable style, the stadium is internationally considered a front-line infrastructure. For example, in 2017 it was the only stadium in Italy chosen to participate in the Stadium of the Year 2017 competition, which considered 27 stadiums worldwide.

The Benito Stirpe PSC Arena is, today, the fourth football stadium infrastructure in Italy that is directly managed by a football club. With more than 16,000 (all covered) seats, 16 Daises, and 10 Sky Boxes (see Figure 1.1), the stadium is a multifunctional infrastructure that can host football matches and other kinds of events associated with entertainment. As an example, in July 2018, it was home to the European Latin Awards, a well-known, international music competition.

From a conceptual point of view, the realization of this stadium is a brilliant example of virtuous *co-evolution* between (at least) two units of analysis, in this case the public (i.e., the Municipality of Frosinone) and private (i.e., the Frosinone Football Club) stakeholder, respectively; for instance, the stadium is built in only 18 months (against 5 years on average), with its "development costs" (i.e., costs per seat) also significantly lower than those of the average.

Figure 1.1 The Benito Stirpe PSC Arena Football Stadium in Frosinone (Italy)

Source: Photographs by the author.

The above introduced, what does the term "co-evolution" mean? As evidenced in the preceding section of this chapter, conceptualizing the adaptation and evolution of enterprises as the result of the dynamic combination between determinism and voluntarism has, over time, become a *quasi*-permanent perspective in management and organization theory. Supported by empirical analyses, ever-refined theoretical routes have been advanced, with an increasing number of scholars (especially from the 1990s) specifically proposing the adoption of co-evolutionary lenses to study the firm/environment relationship. From the beginning, we can state that, in line with most of the concepts explained in this chapter so far, co-evolution – as a theoretical construct – also owes its roots to natural sciences, especially in its most recent approaches. In this regard, as recently argued by Laland et al. (2014: 161–162):

> "We believe that the extended evolutionary synthesis will shed new light on how evolution works. We hold that organisms are constructed in development, not simply 'programmed' to develop by genes. Living things do not evolve to fit into pre-existing environments, but co-construct and co-evolve with their environments, in the process changing the structure of ecosystems".[3]

In general, natural sciences conceive co-evolution as the contemporaneous evolutionary change witnessed by two (species of) living organisms because of their interaction and respective adaptation pressures (e.g., Nuismer, 2017). In particular, to be considered as *really* co-evolutionary this change needs to respect all these three conditions (Janzen, 1980; Abatecola et al., 2020a): (i) it has to be *specific*, which means that one organism "A" changes because of the particular behaviour of one organism "B" (e.g., zebras [A] attempt to escape because lions [B] attack); (ii) it has to be *reciprocal*, which means that not only the ways through which lions decide their attack strategies depend on their observation of the ways through which zebras attempt to escape but also that the ways through which zebras decide their escape strategies depend on their observation of the ways through which lions attack; (iii) it has to be *simultaneous*, which means that, if individually observed, the change affecting the behaviour both of lions and zebras has to occur at the same time.

The above explained in terms of distinctive conditions, in natural sciences, co-evolution has been generally observed to occur according to the following three main configurations (Thompson, 1982; Breslin et al., 2021): (i) *antagonistic*, which, as – for example – in the case of predators and preys, substantiates the situation of a dichotomous and hostile co-evolving relationship between two (species of) organisms (predators try to select out preys and preys try to avoid being selected out by predators); (ii) *competitive*, which, as – for example – in the case of lions and tigers struggling for the same food, substantiates the situation of two co-evolving (species of) organisms in direct rivalry for the appropriation of the same limited resources; and (iii) *mutualistic*, which, as – for example – in the case of bees and flowers (or bacteria and humans), substantiates the situation in which the relationship between two co-evolving (species of) organisms provides benefits to both. Relatedly, while each of these three configurations conceptually represents a co-evolutionary mode *per se*, over time this mode can change; for example, from mutualistic to antagonistic and then back to mutualistic, or from competitive to mutualistic and then to antagonistic.

In management and organization theory, co-evolution has been initially conceived as the collective change resulting from the interaction between strategic free will and environmental pressures (e.g., Baum and Singh, 1994), with the latter both at the industry and socio-economic levels. In particular, from the different kinds of analysis produced over time, some general, conceptual properties of co-evolution have been derived (Lewin and Volberda, 1999). Among those, what is key is that co-evolution has a *multi-level,* long-term nature, based on interdependence and reciprocal feedback (e.g., Brusoni and Prencipe, 2006; Gatti et al., 2015). For example, if one firm (as a whole) is taken as the unit of analysis (e.g. Weber, 2017), co-evolution has to be considered that change not only affecting this unit but also its industry and institutional environment (with the change being the result of all their collective interaction). This multi-level nature also holds if one, instead, looks inside any organizational structure (e.g., Sandhu and Kulik, 2019), with a focus, for example, on the interaction between the governance, management, and operations levels.

On this basis, a distinction can be made between "macro" and "micro" co-evolution (McKelvey, 1997). The former, on the one hand, can be conceived as that occurring between enterprises and their external environment (for example, the growth of the Gross Domestic Product of one country is generally the combined result of how companies in that country perform and of how, in parallel, that country facilitates, or obstacles, their performance); the latter, on the other hand, can be conceptualized as that regarding the intra-organizational resources and capabilities (for example, product innovation is generally the result of the co-evolutionary process of interaction between the Research & Development, Marketing, and Manufacturing departments). Relatedly, in natural sciences, *direct* co-evolution refers to the reciprocal change of two specific units of analysis in any given ecosystem, while *diffuse* co-evolution regards the change affecting all the units in that ecosystem (Janzen, 1980). As for business, for instance, if we go back to our initial example – in this section – regarding the construction of the football stadium, the former kind of co-evolutionary observation would only focus on the reciprocal interaction between (and behavioural change of) the Municipality and the football club. The latter kind of observation, instead, would also include all the other stakeholders influencing (and influenced by) the project, such as the financial institutions, supporters, media, and territory as a whole (Abatecola et al., 2020b).

In the management and organization theory literature, studies on co-evolution have embraced many different lines of research settings over time. Qualitative research methods have been largely predominant, with observation periods ranging from some years to decades, and (even) centuries. The research designs, at the same time, have also witnessed (at least) one element gradually changing. In particular, while, at the beginning, firms were taken as the primary unit of analysis (e.g., Van den Bosch et al., 1999), over time this unit has been progressively accompanied by a number of others observed, these including (but not limited to): artefacts (e.g., Fleck, 2000), capabilities (e.g., Jacobides and Winter, 2005), environmental regulations (e.g., Rizzi and Frey, 2014), leadership (e.g., Spisak et al., 2015), technology (e.g., Grodal et al., 2015), industries (e.g. Paniccia and Baiocco, 2021), socio-economic systems (e.g., Almudi and Fatas-Villafranca, 2021), and business networks (e.g., Cristofaro et al., 2024). Relatedly, which appears as a further connection to what explained in this chapter so far, it seems worth noticing that some studies have also advanced conceptual trajectories in which co-evolution is attempted to be specifically grounded on the evolutionary mechanisms of variation, selection, and retention. In this regard, for example, one of the most pioneering studies is that by John Peter Murmann (2003), which concentrates on analysing how the synthetic dye industry evolved from 1856 until World

War I. As a key component, the study combines the national industry (i.e., UK, Germany, France, and the US) perspective with both the technology (i.e., the introduction of the synthetic dye) and national institutional (i.e., educational systems and patent laws) perspectives. Specifically, on the one hand, Murmann uses variation, selection, and retention to explicate the evolutionary change affecting both the synthetic die industry and its institutional environment; on the other hand, he also shows how the mutual interaction between the two impacted on their change when individually considered.[4]

1.6 Summary

Also using examples from the practice of business, this chapter has attempted to provide both scholars and practitioners with an overview regarding the various lines of inquiry and associated theoretical conjectures developed around the enterprise evolution research field over time. Drawing on natural sciences (e.g., Eldredge et al., 2016), this chapter has begun with the effort to trace a conceptual perimeter for the field; it has then moved to consider the determinism/voluntarism dichotomy and, subsequently, the flourishing of the dialectical and (later) co-evolutionary perspectives about the adaptation and evolution of enterprises. Among those emerged, the main takeaways could be summarized as follows.

First, this chapter has highlighted that the perimeter of enterprise evolution, as a per se research area, has been increasing considerably over time and is currently significant. As an example, in the previous pages the chapter has raised two simple questions, i.e., "how enterprises *evolve*", and (relatedly) "how enterprises *adapt*". In this regard, as this chapter has explained, a number of paradigms of thought have offered suggestive interpretations about how to address these questions. As also explained, some of these paradigms have been juxtaposing for a long time (Van de Ven and Poole, 2005), with this juxtaposition substantially ascribing primacy to the environmental constraints on the one hand (i.e., determinism) or to the strategic free will on the other hand (i.e., voluntarism).

Second, the chapter has explicated that, in terms of current research avenues within the area, the juxtaposition between determinism and voluntarism in shaping the adaptation and evolution of enterprises seemingly represents the past (e.g., Audretsch et al., 2024). In fact, as the chapter has explicated, an important conciliation has been offered by dialectical and co-evolutionary thinking, whose constant nurturing in the future is also auspicated (Chapter 4 will expand on this point). For example, this chapter has highlighted that while qualitative research methods have been largely predominant in co-evolutionary research, quantitative methods are still scant. Thus, analyses able to combine both these methods could probably constitute an important *plus*.

In conclusion, with no ambition of resulting exhaustive in terms of perspectives and concepts analysed, this chapter can provide a contribution which is both conceptual and methodological. From a conceptual point of view, this chapter can help recognize what (and why) certain schools of thought developed over time can be considered *in* the enterprise evolution research field. At the same time, from a methodological point of view, the chapter can help distinguish the main differences and similarities between and among these schools.

Notes

1 Also assuming a macro-perspective, over time the approach developed by "evolutionary economics" has, instead, also drawn on the Schumpeterian assumption of "creative destruction" as its conceptual basis (e.g., Dosi, 2023).

2 Likewise, Arthur Bedeian (1990) proposes an "inter-actionist", organizational learning-based perspective, as a possible integration of the framework by Hrebiniak and Joyce.

3 In their landmark commentary on *Nature*, Laland et al. (2014) offer a point-counterpoint argument on the main differences between the "modern" (e.g., Huxley, 1942) and the "extended" (e.g., Pigliucci and Müller, 2010) evolutionary synthesis, with the former, for example, gene-centred and the latter organism-centred.

4 Subsequently, Murmann (2013) also explains what determinants (e.g., working capital exchange, commercial ties, and lobbying) influenced how the synthetic dye industry has evolved. In particular, he explains how, through their reciprocal interaction, these determinants affected the process of variation, selection, and retention.

References

Abatecola, G. (2012). 'Organizational adaptation. An update'. *International Journal of Organizational Analysis*, **20**(3), 274–293.

Abatecola, G. (2014). 'Research in organizational evolution. What comes next?' *European Management Journal*, **32**(3), 434–443.

Abatecola, G., Breslin, D. and Kask, J. (2020a). 'Do organizations really co-evolve? Problematizing co-evolutionary change in management and organization studies'. *Technological Forecasting and Social Change*, **155**, 119964.

Abatecola, G., Mari, M. and Poggesi, S. (2020b). 'How can virtuous real estate public-private partnerships be developed? Towards a co-evolutionary perspective'. *Cities*, **107**, 102896.

Aldrich, H.E., Ruef, M. and Lippmann, S. (2020). *Organizations evolving* (3rd edition). Edward Elgar.

Almudi, I. and Fatas-Villafranca, F. (2021). *Co-evolution in economic systems*. Cambridge University Press.

Astley, W.G. and Van de Ven, A.H. (1983). 'Central perspectives and debates in organization theory'. *Administrative Science Quarterly*, **28**(2), 245–273.

Audretsch, D.B., Aronica, M., Belitski, M. and Piacentino, D. (2024). 'Natural selection or strategic adaptation? Entrepreneurial digital technologies and survival of the species'. *Journal of Technology Transfer*, **49**, 1631–1659.

Baum, J.A.C. and Singh, J.V. (1994). 'Organization-environment co-evolution'. In J.A.C. Baum and J.V. Singh (Eds.), *Evolutionary dynamics of organizations*. Oxford University Press, 379–402.

Becker, M.C. (2004). 'Organizational routines: A review of the literature'. *Industrial and Corporate Change*, **13**(4), 643–677.

Bedeian, A.G. (1990). 'Choice and determinism. A comment'. *Strategic Management Journal*, **11**(7), 571–573.

Benson, J.K. (1977). 'Organizations: A dialectical view'. *Administrative Science Quarterly*, **22**(1), 1–21.

Bourgeois, L.J. III (1984). 'Strategic management and determinism'. *Academy of Management Review*, **9**(4), 586–596.

Breslin, D. (2011). 'Reviewing a generalized Darwinist approach to studying socio-economic change'. *International Journal of Management Reviews*, **13**(2), 218–235.

Breslin, D., Kask, J., Schlaile, M. and Abatecola, G. (2021). 'Developing a co-evolutionary account of innovation ecosystems'. *Industrial Marketing Management*, **98**, 59–68.

Brusoni, S. and Prencipe, A. (2006). 'Making design rules: A multidomain perspective'. *Organization Science*, **17**(2), 179–189.

Burgelman, R.A. (1991). 'Intra-organizational ecology of strategy making and organizational adaptation: Theory and field research'. *Organization Science*, **2**(3), 239–262.

Burgelman, R.A., Snihur, Y. and Thomas, L.D.W. (2023). *Strategy-making and organizational evolution. A managerial agency perspective*. Cambridge University Press.

Cafferata, R. (2016). 'Darwinist connections between the systemness of social organizations and their evolution'. *Journal of Management and Governance*, **20**(1), 19–44.

Cafferata, R. (2022). *Management in adattamento. Tra razionalità economica, evoluzione ed imperfezione dei sistemi* (3rd edition). Il Mulino.

Campbell, D. (1965). 'Variation, selection and retention in sociocultural evolution'. In H.R. Barringer, G.I. Blanksten and R.W. Mack (Eds.), *Social change in developing areas: A reinterpretation of evolutionary theory*. Schenkman, 19–49.

Child, J. (1972). 'Organizational structure, environment and performance: The role of strategic choice'. *Sociology*, **6**(1), 1–22.

Child, J. (1997). 'Strategic choice in the analysis of action, structure, organization and the environment: Retrospect and prospect'. *Organization Studies*, **18**(1), 43–76.

Cristofaro, M., Abatecola, G. and Kask, J. (2024). 'Business network paradoxes: A literature review and co-evolutionary perspective'. *Industrial Marketing Management*, **120**, 115–131.

Cyert, R.M. and March, J.G. (1963). *A behavioural theory of the firm*. Prentice-Hall.

Darwin, C.R. (1859). *On the origin of species by means of natural selection or the preservation of favoured races in the struggle for life*. John Murray.

Dawkins, R. (1976). *The selfish gene*. Oxford University Press.

Dess, G.G. and Beard, D.W. (1984). 'Dimensions of organizational task environments'. *Administrative Science Quarterly*, **29**(1), 52–73.

Di Maggio, P.J. and Powell, W.W. (1983). 'The iron cage revisited: Institutional isomorphism and collective rationality in organizational fields'. *American Sociological Review*, **48**(2), 147–160.

Dosi, G. (2023). *The foundation of complex evolving economics. Part one: Innovation, organization, and industrial dynamics*. Oxford University Press.

Durand, R. (2006). *Organizational evolution and strategic management*. Sage.

Eldredge, N. and Gould, S.J. (1972). 'Punctuated equilibria: An alternative to phyletic gradualism'. In T.J.M. Schopf (Ed.), *Models in paleobiology*. Freeman, Cooper, 82–115.

Eldredge, N., Pievani, T., Serrelli, E. and Temkin, I. (Eds., 2016). *Evolutionary theory. A hierarchical perspective*. Chicago University Press.

Fleck, J. (2000). 'Artefact ↔ activity: The co-evolution of artefacts, knowledge and organization in technological innovation'. In J. Ziman (Ed.), *Technological innovation as an evolutionary process*. Cambridge University Press, 248–266.

Foss, N.J. (2021). 'The impact of the Covid-19 pandemic on firm's organizational designs'. *Journal of Management Studies*, **58**(1), 270–274.

Gatti, C., Volpe, L. and Vagnani, G. (2015). 'Interdependence among productive activities: Implications for exploration and exploitation'. *Journal of Business Research*, **68**(3), 711–722.

Gill, J. and Price, I. (2022). 'A meme-based research programme for management and organization studies'. *International Journal of Management Reviews*, **24**(3), 415–432.

Gowdy, J.E., Dollimore, D.E., Wilson, D.S. and Witt, U. (2013). 'Economic cosmology and the evolutionary challenge'. *Journal of Economic Behaviour and Organization*, **90**, S11–S20.

Grandinetti, R. (2018). 'Is organizational evolution Darwinian and/or Lamarckian?'. *International Journal of Organizational Analysis*, **26**(5), 858–874.

Grodal, S., Gotsopoulos, A. and Suarez, F. (2015). 'The co-evolution of technologies and categories during industry emergence'. *Academy of Management Review*, **40**(3), 420–445.

Hambrick, D.C. and Mason, P.A. (1984). 'Upper echelons: The organization as a reflection of its top managers'. *Academy of Management Review*, **9**(2), 193–206.

Hannan, M.T. and Freeman, J.H. (1977). 'The population ecology of organizations'. *American Journal of Sociology*, **82**(5), 929–964.

Hegel, G.W.F. (1807). *Phänomenologie des Geistes*.

Hodgson, G.M. and Knudsen, T. (2010). *Darwin's conjecture: The search for general principles of social and economic evolution*. University of Chicago Press.

Hrebiniak, L.G. and Joyce, W.F (1985). 'Organizational adaptation: Strategic choice and environmental determinism'. *Administrative Science Quarterly*, **30**(3), 336–349.

Hull, D.L. (1988). *Science as a process*. University of Chicago Press.

Huxley, J. (1942). *Evolution: The modern synthesis*. Harper & Brothers.

Jacobides, M.G. and Winter, S.G. (2005). 'The co-evolution of capabilities and transaction costs: Explaining the institutional structure of production'. *Strategic Management Journal*, **26**(5), 395–413.

Janzen, D. (1980). 'When is it coevolution?'. *Evolution*, **34**(3), 611–612.

Johansson, T. and Kask, J. (2013). 'On the promise and premises of a Darwinian theory in research on business relationships'. *Industrial Marketing Management*, **42**(3), 306–315.

Laland, K., Uller, T., Feldman, M., Sterelny, K., Muller, G.B., Moczek, A., Jablonka, E., Odling-Smee, J., Wray, G.A., Hoekstra, H.E., Futuyma, D.J., Lenski, R.E., Mackay, T.F.C., Schluter, D. and Strassmann, J.E. (2014). 'Does evolutionary theory need a rethink?' *Nature*, **514**, 161–164.

Lawless, M.W. and Finch, L.K. (1989). 'Choice and determinism: A test of Hrebiniak and Joyce's framework on strategy-environment fit'. *Strategic Management Journal*, **10**(4), 351–365.

Lawrence, P.R. and Lorsch, J.W. (1967). *Organization and environment: Managing differentiation and integration.* Harvard Business School Press.

Levinthal, D.A. (2021). *Evolutionary processes and organizational adaptation: A Mendelian perspective on strategic management.* Oxford University Press.

Lewin, A.Y. and Volberda, H.K. (1999). 'Prolegomena on co-evolution: A framework for research on strategy and new organizational forms'. *Organization Science*, **10**(5), 519–534.

Lewontin, R.C. (1978). 'Adaptation'. *Scientific American*, **239**(3), 212–28.

Lewontin, R.C. (1983). 'The organism as the subject and object of evolution'. *Scientia*, **118**, 63–82.

Malerba, F. and Lee, K. (2017). 'An evolutionary perspective on economic catch-up by latecomers'. *Industrial and Corporate Change*, **30**(4) 986–1010.

McCarthy, I.P., Collard, M. and Johnson, M. (2017). 'Adaptive organizational resilience: An evolutionary perspective'. *Current Opinion in Environmental Sustainability*, **28**, 33–40.

McKelvey, B. (1997). 'Quasi-natural organization science'. *Organization Science*, **8**(4), 352–380.

Miller, D. (1986). 'Configurations of strategy and structure: Towards a synthesis'. *Strategic Management Journal*, **7**(3), 233–249.

Murmann, J.P. (2003). *Knowledge and competitive advantage: The co-evolution of firms, technology and national institutions.* Cambridge University Press.

Murmann, J.P. (2013). 'The co-evolution of industries and important features of their environments'. *Organization Science*, **24**(1), 58–78.

Nelson, R.R. and Winter, S.G. (1982). *An evolutionary theory of economic change.* Harvard University Press.

Nuismer, S.L. (2017). *Introduction to coevolutionary theory.* W.H. Freeman.

Osborn, H.F. (1905). 'Tyrannosaurus and other Cretaceous carnivorous dinosaurs'. *Bulletin of the American Museum of Natural History*, **21**, 259–265.

Paniccia, P.M.A. and Baiocco, S. (2021). 'Interpreting sustainable agritourism through co-evolution of social organizations'. *Journal of Sustainable Tourism*, **29**(1), 87–105.

Penrose, E.T. (1959). *The theory of the growth of the firm.* Oxford University Press.

Pettigrew, A.M. (1987). 'Context and action in the transformation of the firm'. *Journal of Management Studies*, **24**(6), 649–670.

Phelps, R., Adams, R. and Bessant, J. (2007). 'Life cycles of growing organizations: A review with implications for knowledge and learning'. *International Journal of Management Reviews*, **9**(1), 1–30.

Pigliucci, M. and Müller, G.B. (Eds., 2010). *Evolution, the extended synthesis.* MIT Press.

Porter, M.E. (1985). *Competitive advantage. Creating and sustaining superior performance.* Free Press.

Reydon, T.A.C. and Scholz, M. (2009). 'Why organizational ecology is not a Darwinian research program'. *Philosophy of the Social Sciences*, **39**(3), 408–439.

Rizzi, F. and Frey, M. (2014). 'Sustainable co-evolution of environmental regulation and oligopolies: Moving towards a managerial theory of meta-organisational approaches'. *International Journal of Innovation and Sustainable Development*, **8**(3), 270–289.

Romanelli, E. and Tushman, M.L. (1994). 'Organizational transformation as punctuated equilibrium: An empirical test'. *Academy of Management Journal*, **37**(5), 1141–1166.

Sandhu, S. and Kulik, C. (2019). 'Shaping and being shaped: How organizational structure and managerial discretion co-evolve in new managerial roles'. *Administrative Science Quarterly*, **64(**3), 619–658.

Sarta, A., Durand, R. and Vergne, J.-P. (2021). 'Organizational adaptation'. *Journal of Management*, **47**(1), 43–75.

Schlaile, M. (Ed., 2021). *Memetics and evolutionary economics. To boldly go where no meme has gone before*. Springer.

Simon, H.A. (1947). *Administrative behaviour. A study of decision-making processes in administrative organization*. Macmillan.

Spisak, B., O'Brien, M., Nicholson, N. and van Vugt, M. (2015). 'Niche construction and the evolution of leadership'. *Academy of Management Review*, **40**(2), 291–306.

Stoelhorst, J.W. (2008). 'The explanatory logic and ontological commitment of generalized Darwinism'. *Journal of Economic Methodology*, **15**(4), 343–363.

Thompson, J. (1982). *Interaction and coevolution*. University of Chicago Press.

Van de Ven, A.H. and Poole, M.S. (1995). 'Explaining development and change in organizations'. *Academy of Management Review*, **20**(3), 510–541.

Van de Ven, A.H. and Poole, M.S. (2005). 'Alternative approaches for studying organizational change'. *Organization Studies*, **26**(9), 1377–1404.

Van den Bosch, F.A.J., Volberda, H.K. and de Boer, M. (1999). 'Co-evolution of firm absorptive capacity and knowledge environment: Organizational forms and combinative capabilities'. *Organization Science*, **10**(5), 551–568.

Weber, L. (2017). 'A sociocognitive view of repeated interfirm exchanges: How the co-evolution of trust and learning impacts subsequent contracts'. *Organization Science*, **28**(4), 744–759.

Weick, K.E. (1969). *The social psychology of organizing*. Addison-Wesley.

Whittington, R. (1988). 'Environmental structure and theories of strategic choice'. *Journal of Management Studies*, **25(**6), 521–536.

2 Enterprise early survival or mortality

2.1 Introduction

How can enterprises survive early mortality? Assuming a critical, global perspective, the question still today is not whether enterprises die young or not. In fact, despite what (unfortunately) remain as exceptions, average data show that early mortality is high for new ventures; in the United States, for example, about one start-up out of two continues to fail by the end of its fifth year of existence (US Bureau of Labor Statistics, 2024).

In the 1960s, the famous American sociologist Arthur Stinchcombe (1965) coins the term "liability of newness" to explain the Darwinian *struggle for survival* (see Chapter 1, pp. 3–4) between newborn and older enterprises, i.e., to explain the rationale behind the disadvantages that start-ups face against their mature counterparts. As Stinchcombe advances, one key element featuring newness is the lack of *trust*, from which start-ups suffer in different ways. At the beginning, for example, trust is missing among the start-ups' participants and often translates into low performance. When discussing this with students, I often use the example of a football team in which most of the players are new (and, sometimes, even the coach). How many matches does the team initially lose? Indeed, that is still not a *team* in the most vivid sense! In parallel, trust is also often missing for what concerns the start-ups' products (goods and/or services). How can consumers like and buy the products of a new player if they substantially do not know it? Many consumers tend to go to the same restaurants and retail shops for their everyday purchases. Likewise, many companies use particular suppliers for extended periods of time due to familiarity and institutional knowledge, among other variables. To overcome this barrier, new companies need to demonstrate their supposed, superior value and utility. Finally, and relatedly, trust also impacts equity lending. People tend to do business with those they know, and like. Likewise, financial institutions seemingly tend to provide better rates to established entities compared to new players.

Also drawing on the examples above, it seems clear that the ideas developed by Stinchcombe about early survival (or mortality) processes have

DOI: 10.4324/9781003412663-2

significantly contributed to the development of the enterprise evolution research field. In particular, with its perceived novelty and importance soon arising, from the 1970s, the *liability* stream of research starts to be growingly acknowledged and considered in the literature. For example, the population ecology school of thought (Hannan and Freeman, 1977), whose main tenets we have explained in Chapter 1 (p. 4), develops its main underpinnings by considering the liability of newness as an important, starting building block to elaborate on the birth and death rates of enterprises.

The above introduced, this chapter aims to explain how the liability stream of research has progressed over time and what legacy the pioneering ideas by Stinchcombe still constitute for the research and practice around enterprise evolution. In this regard, the structure of the chapter is as follows. First, this chapter provides an initial overview of the liability of newness as a theoretical construct. Second, this chapter continues by illustrating how, following newness, a number of important *first-wave* concepts, such as "smallness", "adolescence", and "aging", have been subsequently raised in the study of the birth and death rates of enterprises. Third, this chapter focuses on what we might consider *second-wave* newness-related constructs, such as "foreignness", "ethnicity", and "identity/conformity/differentiation". Fourth, with a focus on the construct known as "imprinting", this chapter discusses what value-added Stinchcombe's legacy can still provide to our understanding of how enterprises evolve and survive. Summary and takeaways for scholars, practitioners, and students conclude this chapter.

2.2 Enterprises die new. Why?

Six decades after its introduction, and although theoretically integrated over time, the liability of newness still seems problematic for many new entrants. We could thus argue that key is how to countervail this liability. In this regard, while, in terms of entrepreneurial, managerial, and policy-making implications, there still appears to be no *magic formula*, the two following points below may be, for example, considered from the beginning:

i *understand market needs*: often times there is a disconnect between the entrepreneur's perception of market demand and reality (e.g., Murphy, 2011). New services, offerings, and products need to fulfil a genuine market demand that provides social value. For example, as recent data from CB Insights (2021) also show, almost the majority of failed start-ups in the US still fell short in this area;

ii *be distinctive*: if we consider electric cars, to date this kind of vehicle still does not seem totally competitive in terms of pricing. But, there is a very good chance that government regulations and changes in the production process will upend this. If this happens, it would mean that, about 20 years ago, Elon Musk identified an opportunity through Tesla that 99.9% of the auto industry failed to see in advance. On this side, I always remember that three brilliant former students of my Enterprise Evolution course at the Tor Vergata University of Rome also caught the potential of Tesla at that time. During a project-work session, when presenting the company to their classmates, they figured out Tesla as one of the most innovative start-ups to "watch". At that time, Tesla was mostly unknown to many!

On this premise, Stinchcombe has undoubtedly contributed significantly to social sciences (e.g., Lounsbury and Ventresca, 2002), with his theoretical and empirical research drawing on a number of heterogeneous social observations (e.g., 2005), such as those regarding conflicts in the school workplace, organizational expertise and industry performance, agriculture, offshore oil exploration, and financial industries. In 1965, Stinchcombe wrote the essay entitled *Social Structure and Organizations*, which soon assumed momentum. With the core of this piece of research around the question of why organizations come to light, evolve, and eventually fail, he develops the "liability of newness" construct. As a key building block, the liability of newness maintains that mortality rates are expected to be high in the first years of the firms' life cycle (and, under certain circumstances, are then expected to decline). Interestingly, in 1965 another landmark piece of research was published, which was *The Causal Texture of Organizational Environments* written by Frederick Emery and Eric Trist (who are commonly known as the fathers of the concept of "socio-technical systems"). In this article, the study of how organizations evolve in turbulent industry contexts has more than one aspect in common with the ideas about enterprise early mortality developed by Stinchcombe.

The ideas embedded in the liability of newness conceptualization constitute an important input to the theoretical speculations, of that time, around the birth and death of enterprises. In particular, the liability of newness leads both scholars and practitioners to focus no longer only on the question of why and how new entrepreneurial businesses can arise but also on the question of why and how these new businesses can fail. According to Stinchcombe, the performance of newborn firms is, on average, low because, at the beginning of their existence, new players witness the absence of *experience* from various aspects. For example, when players are new, work roles and processes have yet to be established in a way that can prove to be ultimately satisfactory. Accordingly, the system of human relations and interdependencies, including effective and efficient rewards, penalties, and sanctions, still needs to be tested. Countervailing all these lacks is clearly time-consuming and this is why, at least at the beginning, conflicts and, more in general, performance inefficiencies result in being an almost always physiological component of the new players' life (1965: 148). In this regard, a key determinant for early survival is constituted by the capability, in general, to constantly increase the experience learning curve (e.g., Zollo and Winter, 2002) and by that, in particular, to establish responsible and well-operating social routines (e.g., Feldman and Pentland, 2003).

As anticipated at the beginning of this chapter, Stinchcombe also points out that one another main competitive disadvantage of newborn enterprises (if compared to their mature counterparts) is that, at the beginning, trust is missing at different levels. In other words, newborn firms need to connect with a number of stakeholders with which they are not so much familiar, including stakeholders both at the *task* (e.g., in the upstream and/or downstream supply chain) and *general* (e.g., governments and/or financial institutions) environment levels (1965: 150). It is clear that to increase their survival chances, newborn enterprises need to develop stable ties with all these key stakeholders, with reciprocal trust serving as a *conditio sine qua non* (e.g., Delbufalo, 2012; La Rocca et al., 2019). However, as Stinchcombe also asserts, the passing of *time* comes to be another physiological condition to have this trust shift into the formal establishment of long-term collaborations. As introduced above, this is why, in the perspective of the liability of newness, the relationship between age and failure rates is, in principle, assumed to be negative. Relatedly, Stinchcombe highlights that building trust is important not only at the external level, i.e., in terms of the relationship between newborn enterprises and their environmental stakeholders; according to the American sociologist, developing trust results key also at the internal level, i.e. in terms of human relationships within the organizational boundaries. In particular, as in the example of the football team in the introduction to this chapter, the lack of intra-organizational trust at the beginning of the organizational life cycle is almost physiological; it is an antecedent of conflicts and, in turn, of low performance. With the passing of time (e.g., Shipp and Jansen, 2021), trust tends to increase within the organizational human subgroups; this fosters the development of dynamic capabilities (Teece et al., 1997) and, as a consequence, performance can increase.

All the above explained, Stinchcombe also argues that, although the focus of the liability of newness is on enterprises at the individual level, its main tenets could be also applied to the study of entire sets of firms featured by analogous characteristics. On this basis, and as anticipated in the introduction to this chapter, the study of the potential relationship between the liability of newness and the main population ecology underpinnings developed in the late 1970s (Hannan and Freeman, 1977) becomes more than a recurring theme in the analyses performed, in the 1980s, under the lenses of this school of thought. In particular, one main research effort of ecologists is that of verifying the coherence of the liability of newness,[1] which finds general support in a number of industry settings (e.g., Freeman et al., 1983). Ecologists, at the same time, also attempt to study what environmental conditions can countervail the liability of newness and thus foster the birth of start-ups. One key element emerging here is that the environmental buffers increase when the "legitimization" level of a population increases (e.g., Wievel and Hunter, 1985). In this regard, ecologists have seen legitimization as a cognitive process through which an *individual* organizational behaviour becomes a behavioural model accepted at the ecosystem level (e.g., Singh et al., 1986). At the same time, recent research has advanced that the ecosystems' legitimization process can also be the consequence of the *collective* action of its heterogeneous participants (Thomas and Ritala, 2022).

2.3 Enterprises die new. Really?

Unicorns, as we know, are mythological creatures commonly depicted as similar to white horses, with a straight, spiral-shaped horn in the middle of their forehead constituting their most distinctive feature. In popular belief, these legendary, rare creatures are associated with particular "capabilities", such as wisdom, purity, and elegance. When considering the business world, these capabilities – together with rarity – also *somewhat* distinguish the so-called "Unicorn" start-ups from other (more common) entrepreneurial species. In fact, Unicorns, as we also know, are rare (and in many cases also famous) start-ups with a market value equal to over US$1 billion before the Initial Public Offering, which are said to belong to an exclusive billion-dollar start-up "club" (Lee, 2013).

The Unicorns' Club is exclusive because, to date, only circa 1,250 active Unicorns exist worldwide, with a collective market value of about $4,000 billion (CB Insights, 2024); these companies are mainly high tech-focused and continue to be primarily located in the US Silicon Valley (although the most valued [May, 2024] is the Chinese ByteDance). In principle, the Unicorns' tremendous market evaluation chiefly derives from the investors' mass perception of these start-ups as market disruptive (e.g., Mollick, 2020), thanks to their platform-based, highly scalable business model (e.g., Tippmann et al., 2023; Cristofaro et al., 2024); in this regard, we could easily think about the "freemium price" distinctive characteristic of world-scale social media platforms, such as Facebook, LinkedIn, Instagram, and Twitter (now X). Although Unicorns (and other forms of high-growth start-ups) constitute a niche in the current entrepreneurial ecosystem (e.g., Aldrich and Ruef, 2018; Zankl and Grimes, 2024), mentioning this niche from the beginning can constitute, we believe, a good rationale to explaining how the liability of newness research stream has evolved over time.

In the 1980s, studying antecedents, obstacles to, and consequences of the liability of newness begins to be primarily connected to observing firm size. In this regard, and especially from the perspective of population ecology, the first research findings suggest that when the dimension of firms is minor, the liability of newness is seemingly significant. In contrast, when the firm size increases, the liability of newness somewhat decreases. Named the "liability of smallness" (Freeman et al., 1983; Aldrich and Auster, 1986), this liability asserts that, if compared to their larger counterparts, small firms substantially suffer from different gaps. For example, they often witness a gap in terms of availability of financial assets, which is primarily the result of the lack of external financial support. At the same time, they often witness a gap in terms of work capabilities, which means that potential employees are more attracted by large enterprises because, in general, they perceive better career opportunities (both in the short and long terms). Accordingly, often they also witness a gap in terms of the possibility of satisfying interest rate payments and those administrative costs necessarily associated with business bureaucracy and laws.

Although separating the effects, of newness and smallness, on early mortality proves challenging (many start-ups are also physiologically small), these two liabilities are generally observed to be co-existing, with the latter soon becoming considered as an antecedent of the former, i.e. *start-ups mostly die young because they are small* (e.g., Wholey and Brittain, 1986). Relatedly, two additional, significant constructs are (more or less in parallel) also introduced, which are the "liability of aging" (Aldrich and Auster, 1986) and the "liability of adolescence" (Levinthal and Fichman, 1988; Brüderl and Schüssler, 1990), respectively. From the beginning, we can assert that the main difference between these two constructs is that, while aging appears as a theoretical juxtaposition (*firms die old*) to the liability of newness, adolescence appears as a theoretical integration (*firms die young, not new*). As an explanatory start, Figure 2.1 attempts to synthesize the evolutionary path conceptually predicted by newness, adolescence, and aging.

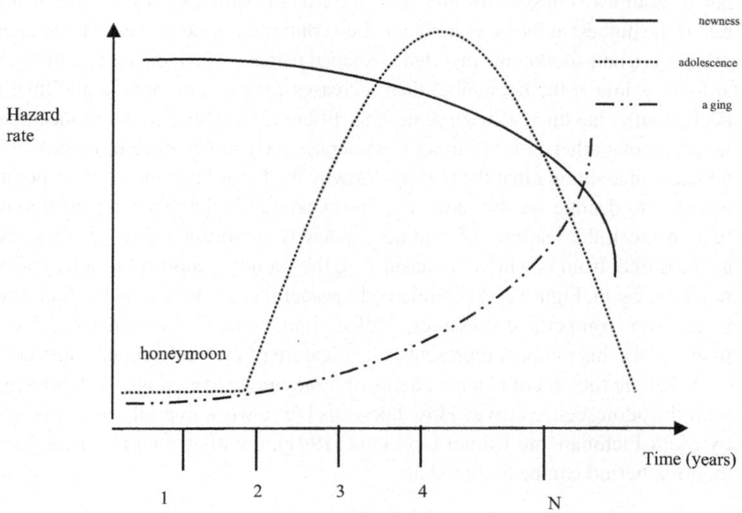

Figure 2.1 Newness, Adolescence, and Aging

Source: Elaboration on Abatecola et al. (2012: 407).

As Figure 2.1 shows, the liability of aging basically assumes that the firm's "hazard rate" (i.e., probability to fail) grows, rather than declines, with its age. As observed, this can – in principle – happen because, over time, those established routines which have once permitted to overcome the liability of newness (and associated smallness) can become, in contrast, sources of structural inertia and of (also potentially associated) "liability of bigness" (Freeman et al., 1983; Aldrich and Auster, 1986); this ultimately translates into environmental *unfit*. In particular, "senescence" and "obsolescence" can constitute two significant, related forms of aging:

> "Senescent processes cause internal decay that increases failure rates independent of environmental conditions and this is a causal effect of aging [...] Obsolescent processes do not directly increase failure rates and thus are not, strictly speaking, direct causal effects of age. Instead, age serves as a proxy for the gap between relatively inert organizations and changing environments (Meyer, 1990). Unlike senescence, obsolescence should not penalize organizations unless they are stressed by changing or turbulent conditions. Senescence is ubiquitous, while obsolescence occurs only during times of environmental upheaval".
>
> (Barron et al., 1994: 387)

The above explained about aging, when considering the theoretical underpinnings of newness and adolescence. Figure 2.1 shows that the "hazard rate" of start-ups is assumed to be partially different; in fact, while newness, as anticipated, assumes a constant decline of the hazard rate, which means that the hazard rate is the highest at the beginning and then continuously decreases, adolescence prospects a non-monotonic inverted U-shaped pattern, which means that the hazard rate is low at the beginning, then increases for a certain period, and finally declines after having reached a peak. This difference highlighted, two conceptual items, among others, merit further consideration: (i) adolescence resonates with newness in assuming that the reasons for why the hazard rate (at a certain point) can start to decline are the same, e.g. (as explained in the preceding section of this chapter), the learning of routines by newly established firms; (ii) adolescence differs from newness in considering the founding moment of a new venture (see, again, Figure 2.1) as a relatively peaceful moment, within the founding stage, from competitive pressures. Called "honeymoon" (Levinthal and Fichman, 1988), this moment represents a key feature of the adolescence construct.

What are the potential antecedents of honeymoon? What is its relationship with the adolescence curve? How does this curve work overall? As explained by Mark Fichman and Daniel Levinthal (1991), the main source for the honeymoon period can be assumed as

> "...an initial stock of assets, which (depending on the particular context) can include favorable prior beliefs, trust, goodwill, financial resources,

> or psychological commitment (p. 442) […] The greater the initial assets of the relationship or organization, the greater will be the buffering from early selection pressures".
>
> (p. 448)

The potential duration of this buffer can vary from some months to some years, with this variance depending on the empowerment effect caused by the assets. Subsequently,

> "…as environmental selection pressures on organizations are brought to bear or mismatches in relationships become evident, the 'hazard rate' increases. As selection pressures continue to weed out unfit organizations or poor matches dissolve, the viability of the surviving matches and organizations increases. Furthermore, adaptation processes and the development of relationship-specific capital make relationships less vulnerable to threats to their survival (England and Farkas, 1986; Levinthal and Fichman, 1988). As a result, the hazard rate should decline with time".
>
> (p. 447)

To explain the conceptual differences and similarities between newness and adolescence with an example from the practice of business, we may think about the opening of a new restaurant. Newness would predict that this new restaurant, substantially without exceptions, would be very likely to fail since the beginning, with the probability of failing physiologically decreasing over time if the governance and management team of the restaurant acquire continuous learning on various business issues. In partial contrast, adolescence would argue that the new restaurant would not necessarily suffer the risk of failure since the very beginning. For example, that restaurant could be opened by founders already well-known in the business world, whose brand (as an asset) could be, at the very beginning, a catalyst for clients themselves. However, with the passing of time, the evolutionary path predicted by adolescence would turn out to be similar to that predicted by newness; in other terms, the founders' brand, in this example, would not result sufficient (per se) to maintain clients. It is like saying that, when the clients' perceptions of the restaurant's novelty end, performance problems for that restaurant would physiologically increase.

With the liability of adolescence also finding interesting support from its start, and its parallel comparison with newness also constantly growing in the 1990s, the conceptual takeaways, in terms of similarities and differences, from the restaurant's example above could be theoretically summarized as clearly done by Andrew Henderson (1999: 283):

> "Common to both the newness and the adolescence perspectives is that the early years of a firm's life are the most hazardous, and failure rates

> eventually decline with age. They differ only about whether failure rates peak at founding or several years later".

In other words, Henderson acknowledges that, if we consider an overall evolutionary path for any given enterprise (i.e., introduction, growth, maturity, and decline), newness and adolescence look like indeed similar; turning back to the example, the restaurant would suffer the highest threats of *selecting out* pressures at the beginning of its existence, rather than in later stages.

2.4 Age is not necessarily important. So, what else?

Having explained the main tenets of newness/smallness, adolescence/honeymoon, and aging/bigness, it is important to highlight that, especially since the second half of the 1990s, there is somewhat a change in the perspective adopted when observing the effects of age on the survival chances of enterprises in general, and of start-ups in particular. Specifically, the main idea gradually becomes that observing age per se is not sufficient to appropriately predict causal effects on organizational mortality rate. Instead, what counts more is understanding whether age increases, or decreases, organizational learning overall.

Of course, one main consequence of the perspective change evidenced above is that the interpretations of newness, adolescence, and aging become *somewhat* more flexible and context-based. In particular, as observed by Joel Baum (1996: 83), "the liabilities of newness, adolescence, and obsolescence can be treated as complementary rather than competing organizational processes if one is able to understand the contingency factors that cause one, the other, or some combination of these models to predominate". In this vein, for example, in a well-known study about the mortality rates of enterprises within the US computer industry, Henderson (1999) observes that newness (specifically, adolescence) or aging (specifically, obsolescence) depend on the kind of technological strategies implemented; obsolescence is associated with "proprietary" strategies, i.e., with strategies drawing on firm-specific core technologies developed from the internal, while adolescence is associated with "standard-based" strategies, i.e., with strategies drawing on open, publicly available core technologies. Relatedly, Henderson also suggests that observing other variables, such as legitimization (see, for example, p. 26 of this chapter), could be key to understand enterprise mortality rates, also in terms of their relationship with age. In this regard, it seems worth of explanation that this suggestion is also connected to a number of liabilities starting to be introduced in parallel and subsequently fostering over time, with the most significant, among others (e.g., Soto-Simeone et al., 2020), outlined below.

Introduced by Srilata Zaheer (1995), the "liability of foreignness" refers to the competitive gap that many enterprises experience when attempting to start a business in a foreign country, with these enterprises sustaining costs which are higher than those sustained by local enterprises. The sources of these additional costs can be different (e.g., logistics, limited knowledge, reputation), with information asymmetry and scarcity of power relationships among the most relevant. This is why, to combat the liability of foreignness, enterprises aiming to set (a branch of) their business abroad should be – in principle – able to: (a) replicate, as much as possible, their own distinctive capabilities (e.g., their brand) in the targeted foreign markets (e.g., Mata and Portugal, 2002); and/or (b) replicate the behaviour of the local market leaders,[2] in a way which somewhat recalls Paul Di Maggio and Woody Powell's 1983 construct of "isomorphism" (see Chapter 1, p. 6).

It is also worth noticing that, subsequently, the foreignness research stream has also witnessed the introduction of the "liability of outsidership" (Johanson and Vahlne, 2009). According to the main tenets surrounding this liability, "a firm's problems and opportunities in international business are becoming less a matter of country-specificity and more one of relationship specificity and network specificity" (Johanson and Vahlne, 2009: 1426). In particular, if we consider the competitive environment as a network of firm relationships, being part of this network allows enterprises to increase their degree of knowledge, perceived trust and thus, in principle, overall performance (e.g., Cepiku et al., 2021). On the contrary, when firms are *outsiders*, i.e., they do not enter this network, obstacles to their performance, such as entry barriers, can arise. Clearly, all this also directly relates back to Stinchcombe's seminal ideas, explained at the beginning of this chapter (p. 25), about the importance, for the start-ups' survival purposes, of developing long-term stable ties; in this regard, "network heritage" (Guercini and Milanesi, 2016) and "status signaling" (Carney and Dieleman, 2024) can also play a role.

The above explained, another liability somewhat considerable among the successors of the "liability of foreignness" can be individuated in the "liability of ethnicity" (Jiang et al., 2016). With a focus on the country of origin of entrepreneurs (e.g., Mata and Alves, 2018; Malki et al., 2020), this liability refers to "the additional costs immigrant-started new ventures experience in their country of residence compared to native-started firms. These costs originate in barriers associated with the primary founder's immigration status" (Jiang et al., 2016: 1286). On average, examples of these barriers have been found to be linguistic problems, limited access to finance, and difficulties in networking with key business and institutional stakeholders. Furthermore, as also highlighted by recent literature (e.g., Mari and Poggesi, 2024), all these barriers seem to be definitely exacerbated when the status of being an immigrant entrepreneur merges with being a woman. In particular, according to the International Organization for Migration (2017), to date immigrant women often suffer from socio-economic challenges, such as unemployment, underemployment, and deskilling.

On the issue above, scholars and policymakers agree that immigrant women entrepreneurs currently experience a particular, concrete double disadvantage, also known as "intersectionality" (Shields, 2008); this disadvantage derives, on the one hand, from their belonging to a national minority (which relates to all the difficulties already highlighted) and, on the other hand, from all the complications connected to their gender, such as limited credit access and obstacles connected to social norms, glass ceiling, etc. (e.g., Jennings and Brush, 2013; De Vita et al., 2014). For example, in their recent study about Hispanic women entrepreneurs, Mindes and Lewin (2023) intervene in the debate around intersectionality, underlining that the existence of multiple and overlaying disadvantages – as in the case of immigrant women entrepreneurs – has an impact greater than that deriving from considering each disadvantage alone. These scholars, in general, stress the need for targeted policies, which, in order to enhance the economic prosperity of countries, should specifically support those individuals who jointly face multiple barriers. In particular, all this is also associated with a potential "liability of womanness" (Yang and Triana, 2019), considered as stemming from the broader gender disparity at the societal level.[3] In this regard, as we detail below, specific considerations about gender-related themes seemingly merit specific highlighting to conclude this section (e.g., Campopiano et al., 2017; Lee and Huang, 2018).

When one given industry is considered,[4] the term "gender imprinting" (see also the next section) is often used to substantiate the "persistence of cultural values, beliefs, norms, and orientations associated, stereotypically, with masculinity or femininity" (Micelotta et al., 2018: 94). On this basis, a recent, suggestive hypothesis is that, when set in gender-dominated industries, start-ups may experience different kinds of liabilities. In particular, the qualitative study conducted by Evelyn Micelotta, Marvin Washington, and Iva Docekalova (2018) regards the introduction of women's professional leagues in the masculine-based Professional Team Sports industry in North America, which includes the National Basketball Association, the Major League Baseball, and the National Football Association. Drawing on the findings of their analysis, these scholars propose three specific, although intertwined liability constructs:

a *identity*, which occurs when a start-up sets vision, mission, and goals which, from a cultural point of view, are not gender-aligned with those prevailing in its industry. For example, when, in 1987, the women's Major Volleyball League was launched, sports media soon commented that the previous launch of other women's team sports, such as basketball and softball, had already been unsuccessful;
b *conformity*, which occurs when a start-up sets its business model in a way that totally aligns with that belonging to the industry. For example, many new women's leagues failed because they attempted to completely

replicate the business model of their male counterparts. While the latter business model mostly based its profitability on the proven success in attracting sponsors, TV contracts, and fans, the former was hardly capable to repeat this success;

c *differentiation*, which occurs as a consequence of the failed attempt to consider the specific gender of a start-up's founding team, when this gender is juxtaposed to that prevailing in the industry, as an element of distinction (e.g., a women-led start-up in a masculine industry or vice versa). For example, the game in many women's leagues was marketed as more elegant and technical (although less powerful) than that of their male counterparts, but the former finally ended in simply being perceived as a *weaker* version of the latter: "In basketball, Cheryl Miller is great, but she doesn't compare to Michael Jordan" (Rosenberg, 1987: 53).

To conclude, and as in the case of "foreignness" (from which we have started the second part of this section), we might add here that also all these three interesting kinds of identified gender-related liability seemingly present something which relates back to the "isomorphism" construct (see, again, Chapter 1, p. 6).

2.5 Imprinting. Stinchcombe's legacy?

As business history has often taught, not rarely entrepreneurs become almost totally resistant to change due to feelings of invincibility deriving from periods of past positive performance. For example, some corporate crises that occurred to industry leaders in the 90s, such as Kodak or Nokia, are seemingly the result of a lack of product innovation following large, previous product success. In this regard, one could think about the famous Snake game with the Nokia 3310 mobile phone. Although excellent, how many years has it remained the same without a new version?

The business example above is connected to what we have explained, so far, in terms of the evolution of the liability of the newness research stream. In particular, what emerges from the previous pages of this chapter is that, at the very beginning, the scholarly attention is mostly on the effects of age (and size) on the survival chances of new enterprises; however, we have then also illustrated how, over time, the focus gradually shifts towards the studying of the relationship between new enterprises' survival (or mortality) and aspects, such as foreignness, ethnicity, and gender, more associated with – one could argue – psychological and behavioural components (e.g., Soto-Simeone et al., 2020). This shift seems not casual, especially if we consider, as we explain here, that a relevant behavioural component relatedly characterizes what can also appear one of the most significant conceptual legacies owed to Stinchcombe, i.e., the "imprinting" construct (1965). In particular, the American sociologist maintains that, during their life cycle, firms which have successfully overcome their liability of newness often maintain their founding "imprint" (i.e., core identity, characteristics and, often, also business model) chiefly because "traditionalizing forces, the vesting of interests, and the working out of ideologies may tend to preserve the structure" (p. 169).

Over time, not only Stinchcombe's "imprinting" hypothesis has been largely supported (e.g., Marquis and Tilcsik, 2013; Simsek et al., 2015) but has also significantly contributed to the birth and development of those management studies aimed at understanding path dependence and self-reinforcing decision-making processes in enterprise evolution (e.g., David, 1985; Arthur, 1994). Drawing, again, on Darwin, we know that history in general, and the "principle of inheritance" in particular (see Chapter 1, pp. 3–4) somewhat count to forecast how organisms adapt and evolve. Both at famous conceptual (e.g., Sydow et al., 2009; Vergne and Durand, 2010) and empirical levels (e.g., Dosi, 1982; Tripsas and Gavetti, 2000), scholars have maintained that history counts also to explain how firms adapt. Commonly used to mean "historical causation", the term "path dependence" has generally symbolized all those kinds of *stamping* effects of the past on the behaviour of evolving enterprises (e.g., Marquis and Huang, 2010; Vergne and Durand, 2011).

Specifically, a simple, illustrative explanation of path dependence, self-reinforcing and, even, final decisional *lock-in* could be as follows (e.g., Abatecola, 2014). Start-ups survive Stinchcombe's liability of newness thanks to the implementation of distinctive competencies and routines. As a consequence of their initial survival, these start-ups raise a business culture which self-reinforces as they evolve, especially if their performance continues to be positive across their subsequent evolutionary path. At a certain point, this culture creates a sort of decisional lock-in, which means that firms do not seek alternatives when facing problems and, even when problems are new, inertially tend to activate problem-solving mechanisms which remain always the same (Sydow and Schreyögg, 2013). However, when problems vary, it seems clear that significant challenges can emerge; although the competitive game is different, resistance to change can be more than a consequence, with all the potential negative effects in terms of organizational performance (we can think back to the initial example about Nokia 3310 at the beginning of this section). At the same time, it seems also arguable that a significant source of behavioural self-reinforcing (and associated path dependence) is constituted by a relevant psychological, irrationality-driven component (e.g., Hammond et al., 1998).

As introduced above, the scholarly inquiries about path dependence have also one more than invisible college with those about resistance to change in general and structural inertia in particular (e.g., Stiglitz et al., 2016). In this regard, Michael Hannan and John Freeman have provided literature with landmark (and still influential) understandings of the reasons why inertia can acquire momentum, at a certain point, in the life of enterprises (1984: 149):

> "Some of the factors that generate structural inertia are internal to organizations: these include sunk costs in plant, equipment and the personnel,

> the dynamics of political coalitions, and the tendency for precedents to become normative standards. Others are external. There are legal and other barriers to entry and exit from realms of activity. Exchange relations with other organizations constitute an investment that is not written off lightly. Finally, attempting radical structural change often threatens legitimacy; the loss of institutional supporting may be devastating".

To conclude, also with regard to path dependence, self-reinforcing, and structural inertia *who says that creativity is an enemy of rationality*? Fostering creativity is important also to solve problems (e.g., Roberto, 2019; Harrison et al., 2024). For example, when practicing problem solving skills with the students of my managerial decision-making course, we also devote attention to the well-known "lateral thinking" techniques developed by Edward De Bono (e.g., 1970) during the second half of the past century. As an application from my teaching experience, when approaching a problem from the practice of business, I first ask students to produce a totally rationality-driven SWOT matrix. I then ask them to generate a series of problem solutions starting from the SWOT which they have produced. But, finally, I also ask them to apply lateral thinking. In this case, this means reversing the logical order of items in the SWOT and wondering whether additional decisional alternatives might come to their mind thanks to this new, supposed order. Overall, the number of decisional alternatives emerging generally increases a lot!

2.6 Summary

Using examples from the practice of entrepreneurship, this chapter has attempted to provide both scholars and practitioners with an account of the various lines of inquiry and associated theoretical conjectures, developed around Arthur Stinchcombe's "liability of newness" (1965) research stream over time. This chapter has begun with explaining the main underpinnings featuring this theoretical construct; it has then moved to consider what we could, to date, perceive as *first* (i.e., "smallness", "adolescence", and "aging") and *second wave* (e.g., "foreignness", "ethnicity", "outsidership", and "gender") newness-related concepts subsequently introduced. This chapter has then ended with discussing Stinchcombe's legacy, highlighting how his construct of "imprinting" has become a key component in the study of how enterprises evolve, especially when mechanisms of path dependence and self-reinforcing processes are under observation. Among those emerged, the main takeaways of this chapter could be summarized as follows.

First, from a conceptual point of view, the chapter has highlighted that there is seemingly a difference in the approach gradually adopted when studying the effects of age on the mortality (or survival) of young enterprises. In particular, *first wave* liabilities chiefly consider age per se:

> "So, smaller and younger organizations usually die young. If they grow, it is often at the expense of their autonomy. Bigger and older organizations, in

> contrast, survive more easily, and do so in part by preying on the smaller and younger organizations continually being created all around them".
> (Aldrich and Auster, 1986: 195)

In contrast, since the second half of the 1990s, the approach has become somewhat more *adaptive* and the attention moved towards the understanding of the effects of age on organizational learning; accordingly, the *second wave* liabilities then flourishing become more grounded on psychological and behavioural determinants (Soto-Simeone et al., 2020). We could also add here that this difference in the approach resonates with the conceptualizations of "objective" and "subjective" *time* also developed in management research; while the former conceptualization substantially considers time in terms of age, the latter pays more attention to time in terms of (cumulated) experience (e.g., Paniccia et al., 2024).

Second, which is also related to methods, this chapter has explained that Stinchcombe's legacy is still significant in the entrepreneurship and management field in general, and in the enterprise evolution research stream in particular. To date, firms worldwide mostly continue to die young and the earliest years of their existence continue to appear as the most challenging for their survival across their entire life cycle (e.g., Josefy et al., 2017). Thus, the question is not whether Stinchcombe's "newness" (and newness-related, such as "adolescence") assumptions still prove to be valid. Much more, the question has over time become how to combat newness (e.g., Caputo and Pellegrini, 2019; Kask and Linton, 2023), which is indeed a question that Stinchcombe himself seminally introduced and, especially for what concerns the external environment, attempted to address.[5] In this regard, research has shown that some internal and external factors, such as the quality of the entrepreneurial founding team and the supporting characteristics of the entrepreneurial ecosystem, respectively, can surely constitute a plus (e.g., Startupgenome, 2024). At the same time, it is still claimed that evidence on these factors appears fragmented (e.g., Bellavitis et al., 2020; Coad and Storey, 2021) and more holistic frameworks are needed if scholars, practitioners and policymakers aim to implement a comprehensive *checklist* of how to become a successful entrepreneur (e.g., Dimov, 2017; Benevolo et al., 2021). To this aim, increasing the empirical analyses outside the US and Europe seems also needed (e.g., Saviano et al., 2017; Dobson et al., 2021) because evidence from Western geographical areas continues to appear predominant (Chapter 4 will elaborate on this point).

In conclusion, who will be the next founder of a high-growth start-up? Notwithstanding the importance and impact of Unicorns, gazelles and other high-growth entrepreneurial species (e.g., Cristofaro et al., 2024), we know that, unfortunately, many start-ups still do not succeed in the Darwinian struggle for survival with their more mature counterparts. Through an overview of Arthur Stinchcombe's pioneering ideas, this chapter has provided its readers with foundational insights about why and how this struggle occurs. From a conceptual point of view, this chapter can help understand why (and how) a number of concepts related to enterprise early survival (or mortality) have been developed over time. At the same time, from a methodological point of view, this chapter can help understand which, between and among these concepts, can result as the most appropriate to comprehend the early pressure dynamics characterizing our business and entrepreneurial world.

Notes

1 From a methodological point of view, for example, one challenge soon emerging from the first empirical analyses conducted is that regarding the proper measurement of organizational failure (e.g., Carroll, 1983).
2 Zaheer (1995) finds the latter action to result more difficult than the former.
3 In their interesting US-based study (2005–2011) about the effect of gender on the survival chances of entrepreneurial ventures, Tiantian Yang and María del Carmen Triana (2019) not only find that, in general, women-led start-ups are more likely to fail than their men-led counterparts. Perhaps more surprisingly, they also find that these probabilities to fail even increase when women launch start-ups in industries, such as those belonging to the third sector, which, in contrast, would be typically perceived to be supportive to them.
4 Or even a sport; we may think, for example, to rugby or football (the latter at least until a few years ago).
5 In particular, according to Stinchcombe (1965: 150–153), the following external factors can facilitate the birth and early survival of new enterprises: (i) general literacy and specialized advanced schooling; (ii) urbanization; (iii) money economy; (iv) political revolution; (v) density of social life, including an already rich organizational life.

References

Abatecola, G. (2014). 'Untangling self-reinforcing processes in managerial decision making. Co-evolving heuristics?' *Management Decision*, **52**(2), 934–949.

Abatecola, G., Cafferata, R. and Poggesi, S. (2012). 'Arthur Stinchcombe's *Liability of Newness*. Contribution and Impact of the Construct'. *Journal of Management History*, **18**(4), 402–418.

Aldrich, H.E. and Auster, E.R. (1986). 'Even dwarfs started small: Liabilities of age and size and their strategic implications'. *Research in Organizational Behaviour*, **8**(2), 165–198.

Aldrich, H.E. and Ruef, M. (2018). 'Unicorns, gazelles, and other distractions on the way to understanding real entrepreneurship in the United States'. *Academy of Management Perspectives*, **32**(4), 458–472.

Arthur, W.B. (1994). *Increasing returns and path dependence in the economy*. University of Michigan Press.

Barron, D.N., West, E. and Hannan, M.T. (1994). 'A time to grow and a time to die: Growth and mortality of credit unions in New York City: 1914–1990'. *American Journal of Sociology*, **100**(2), 381–421.

Baum, J.A.C. (1996). 'Organizational ecology'. In S.R. Clegg, C. Hardy and W. Nord (Eds.), *Handbook of organization studies*. Sage, 77–114.

Bellavitis, C., Rietveld, J. and Filatotchev, I. (2020). 'The effects of prior co-investments on the performance of venture capitalist syndicates: A relational agency perspective'. *Strategic Entrepreneurship Journal*, **14**(2), 240–264.

Benevolo, C., Penco, L. and Torre, T. (2021). 'Entrepreneurial decision-making for global strategies: A "heart–head" approach'. *Management Decision*, **59**(5), 1132–1157.

Brüderl, J. and Schüssler, R. (1990). 'Organizational mortality: The liabilities of newness and adolescence'. *Administrative Science Quarterly*, **35**(3), 530–547.

Campopiano, G., De Massis, A., Rinaldi, F.R. and Sciascia, S. (2017). 'Women's involvement in family firms: Progress and challenges for future research'. *Journal of Family Business Strategy*, **8**(4), 200–212.

Caputo, A. and Pellegrini, M.M. (Eds., 2019). *The anatomy of entrepreneurial decisions: Past, present and future research directions*. Springer Nature.

Carney, M. and Dieleman, M. (2024). 'See who I know! Addressing the liabilities of outsidership through status signaling'. *Journal of International Business Studies*, **55**, 377–395.

Carroll, G.R. (1983). 'A stochastic model of organizational mortality: Review and reanalysis'. *Social Science Research*, **12**(4), 303–329.

CB Insights (2021). *The top 12 reasons start-ups fail*. Retrieved from https://www.cbinsights.com/research/report/startup-failure-reasons-top/ (Last access: November 4, 2024).

CB Insights (2024). *The complete list of Unicorn companies*. Retrieved from https://www.cbinsights.com/research-unicorn-companies (Last access: November 4, 2024).

Cepiku, D., Giordano, F., Mastrodascio, M. and Wang, W. (2021). 'What drives network effectiveness? A configurational approach'. *Public Management Review*, **23**(10), 1479–1503.

Coad, A. and Storey, D. (2021). 'Taking the entrepreneur out of entrepreneurship'. *International Journal of Management Reviews*, **23**(4), 541–548.

Cristofaro, M., Abatecola, G., Giannetti, F. and Zannoni, A. (2024). 'The survival of the fastest: Unveiling the determinants of unicorns and gazelles' early success'. *Scandinavian Journal of Management*, **40**(2), 101335.

David, P.A. (1985). 'Clio and the economics of QWERTY'. *American Economic Review*, **75**(2), 332–337.

De Bono, E. (1970). *Lateral thinking. A textbook of creativity*. Penguin Books.

Delbufalo, E. (2012). 'Outcomes of inter-organizational trust in supply chain relationships: A systematic literature review and a meta-analysis of the empirical evidence'. *Supply Chain Management: An International Journal*, **17**(4), 377–402.

De Vita, L., Mari, M. and Poggesi, S. (2014). 'Women entrepreneurs in and from developing countries: evidences from the literature'. *European Management Journal*, **32**(3), 451–460.

Di Maggio, P.J. and Powell, W.W. (1983). 'The iron cage revisited: Institutional isomorphism and collective rationality in organizational fields'. *American Sociological Review*, **48**(2), 147–160.

Dimov, D. (2017). *The reflective entrepreneur*. Routledge.

Dobson, S., Jones, P., Agyapong, D. and Maas, G. (Eds., 2021). *Enterprising Africa: Transformation through entrepreneurship.* Routledge.

Dosi, G. (1982). 'Technological paradigms and technological trajectories: A suggested interpretation of the determinants and directions of technical change'. *Research Policy*, **11**(3), 147–162.

Emery, F.E. and Trist, E.L. (1965). 'The causal texture of organizational environments'. *Human Relations*, **18**(1), 21–32.

England, P. and Farkas, G. (1986). *Households, employment and gender*. Aldine.

Feldman, M.S. and Pentland, B.T. (2003). 'Reconceptualizing organizational routines as a source of flexibility and change'. *Administrative Science Quarterly*, **48**(1), 94–118.

Fichman, M. and Levinthal, D.A. (1991). 'Honeymoons and the liability of adolescence: A new perspective on duration dependence in social and organizational relationships'. *Academy of Management Review*, **16**(2), 442–468.

Freeman, J., Carroll, G.R. and Hannan, M.T. (1983). 'The liability of newness: Age dependence in organizational death rates'. *American Sociological Review*, **48**(5), 692–710.

Guercini, S. and Milanesi, M. (2016). 'Interaction approach and liabilities: A case analysis of start-up firms'. *Journal of Business-to-Business Marketing*, **23**(4), 293–309.

Hammond, J.S. III, Keeney, R.L. and Raiffa, H. (1998). 'The hidden traps of decision making'. *Harvard Business Review*, **76**(5), 47–58.

Hannan, M.T. and Freeman, J.H. (1977). 'The population ecology of organizations'. *American Journal of Sociology*, **82**(5), 929–964.

Hannan, M.T. and Freeman, J.H. (1984). 'Structural inertia and organizational change'. *American Sociological Review*, **49**(2), 149–164.

Harrison, S.H., Hua, M. and Deasy, D. (2024). '*Scar tissue that I wish you saw*: Creativity scars and their impact on creative work'. *Academy of Management Discoveries*, https://doi.org/10.5465/amd.2023.0141.

Henderson, A.D. (1999). 'Firm strategy and age dependence: A contingent view of the liabilities of newness, adolescence and obsolescence'. *Administrative Science Quarterly*, **44**(2), 281–314.

International Organization for Migration (2017). *Migration in the 2030 agenda.* Retrieved from https://www.iom.int/sites/default/files/about-iom/gender/Migration-in-the-2030-Agenda-SDGs-Achieving-Gender-Equality-through-Migration-Governance.pdf (Last access: November 6, 2024).

Jennings, J.E. and Brush, C.G. (2013). 'Research on women entrepreneurs: Challenges to (and from) the broader entrepreneurship literature?'. *Academy of Management Annals*, **7**(1), 663–715.

Jiang, G.H., Kotabe, M., Hamilton, R.D. and Smith, S.W. (2016). 'Early internationalization and the role of immigration in new venture survival'. *International Business Review*, **25**(6), 1285–1296.

Johanson, J. and Vahlne, J.E. (2009). 'The Uppsala internationalization process model revisited: From liability of foreignness to liability of outsidership'. *Journal of International Business Studies*, **40**, 1411–1431.

Josefy, M.A., Harrison, J.S., Sirmon, D.G. and Carnes, C. (2017). 'Living and dying: Synthesizing the literature on firm survival and failure across stages of development'. *Academy of Management Annals*, **11**(2), 770–799.

Kask, J. and Linton, G. (2023). 'Editorial: Five principles for overcoming obstacles in deep-tech startup journeys'. *Journal of Small Business and Enterprise Development*, **30**(1), 1–3.

La Rocca, A., Perna, A., Snehota, I. and Ciabuschi, F. (2019). 'The role of supplier relationships in the development of new business ventures'. *Industrial Marketing Management*, **80**, 149–159.

Lee, A. (2013). *Welcome to the Unicorn club: Learning from billion-dollar start-ups*. Retrieved from https://techcrunch.com/2013/11/02/welcome-to-the-unicorn-club/ (Last access: November, 4, 2024).

Lee, M. and Huang, L. (2018). 'Gender bias, social impact framing, and evaluation of entrepreneurial ventures'. *Organization Science*, **29**(1), 1–16.

Levinthal, D.A. and Fichman, M. (1988). 'Dynamics of interorganizational attachments: Auditor-client relationships'. *Administrative Science Quarterly*, **33**(3), 345–506.

Lounsbury, M. and Ventresca, M.J. (Eds., 2002). *Research in the sociology of organizations, vol 19: Social structure and organizations revisited*. Elsevier.

Malki, B., Uman, T. and Pittino, D. (2020). 'The entrepreneurial financing of the immigrant entrepreneurs: A literature review'. *Small Business Economics*, **58**(3), 1337–1365.

Mari, M. and Poggesi, S. (2024). *Current trends in female entrepreneurship: Innovation and immigration*. Emerald.

Marquis, C. and Huang, Z. (2010). 'Acquisitions as exaptation: The legacy of founding institutions in the US commercial banking industry'. *Academy of Management Journal*, **53**(6), 1141–1473.

Marquis, C. and Tilcsik, A. (2013). 'Imprinting: Toward a multilevel theory'. *Academy of Management Annals*, **7**(1), 193–243.

Mata, J. and Alves, C. (2018). 'The survival of firms founded by immigrants: Institutional distance between home and host country, and experience in the host country'. *Strategic Management Journal*, **39**(11), 2965–2991.

Mata, J. and Portugal, P. (2002). 'The survival of new domestic and foreign-owned firms'. *Strategic Management Journal*, **23**(4), 323–343.

Meyer, M.W. (1990). 'Notes of a skeptic: From organizational ecology to organizational evolution'. In J.V. Singh (Ed.), *Organizational evolution: New directions*. Sage, 298–314.

Micelotta, E., Washington, M. and Docekalova, I. (2018). 'Industry gender imprinting and new venture creation: The liabilities of women's leagues in the sports industry'. *Entrepreneurship Theory and Practice*, **42**(1), 94–128.

Mindes, S.C.H. and Lewin, P. (2023). 'Intersectional dimensions of entrepreneurship among immigrant Hispanic women'. *Journal of Small Business Management*, **62**(5), 2181–2210.

Mollick, E. (2020). *The Unicorn's shadow: Combating the dangerous myths that hold back startups, founders, and investors*. Wharton School Press.

Murphy, P.J. (2011). 'A 2x2 conceptual foundation for entrepreneurial discovery theory'. *Entrepreneurship Theory and Practice*, **35**(2), 359–374.

Paniccia, P.M.A., Abatecola, G. and Baiocco, S. (2024). 'Integrating time and knowledge to understand organizational evolution: Towards a conceptual framework'. *Journal of Knowledge Management*, **18**(11), 62–77.

Roberto, M.A. (2019). *Unlocking creativity: How to solve any problem and make the best decisions by shifting creative mindsets*. John Wiley & Sons.

Rosenberg, S. (1987). 'Psst, Los Angeles has already won the title'. *Los Angeles Times*, May 30, 12.

Saviano, M., Nenci, L. and Caputo, F. (2017). 'The financial gap for women in the MENA region: a systemic perspective'. *Gender in Management*, **32**(3), 203–217.

Shields, S.A. (2008). 'Gender: An intersectionality perspective'. *Sex Roles*, **59**, 301–311.

Shipp, A.J. and Jansen, K.J. (2021). 'The "other" time: A review of the subjective experience of time in organizations'. *Academy of Management Annals*, **15**(1), 299–334.

Simsek, Z., Curtis Fox, B. and Heavey, C. (2015). 'What's past is prologue: A framework, re-view, and future directions for organizational research on imprinting'. *Journal of Management*, **41**(1), 288–317.

Singh, J.V., Tucker, D.J. and House, R.J. (1986). 'Organizational legitimacy and the liability of newness'. *Administrative Science Quarterly*, **31**(2), 171–193.

Soto-Simeone, A., Sirén, C. and Antretter, T. (2020). 'New venture survival: A review and extension'. *International Journal of Management Reviews*, **22**(4), 378–407.

Stiglitz, N., Knudsen, T. and Becker, M.C. (2016). 'Adaptation and inertia in dynamic environments'. *Strategic Management Journal*, **37**(9), 1854–1864.

Startupgenome (2024). *The global startup ecosystem report 2024*. Retrieved from https://startupgenome.com/reports/gser2024 (Last access: November 9, 2024).

Stinchcombe, A.L. (1965). 'Social structure and organizations'. In J. March (Ed.), *Handbook of organizations*. Rand McNally, 142–193.

Stinchcombe, A.L. (2005). *The logic of social research*. University of Chicago Press.

Sydow, J. and Schreyögg, G. (Eds., 2013). *Self-reinforcing processes in and among organizations*. Palgrave Macmillan.

Sydow, J., Schreyögg, G. and Koch, J. (2009). 'Organizational path dependence: Opening the black box'. *Academy of Management Review*, **34**(4), 689–709.

Teece, D.J., Pisano, G. and Shuen, A. (1997). 'Dynamic capabilities and strategic management'. *Strategic Management Journal*, **18**(7), 509–533.

Thomas, L.D.W. and Ritala, P. (2022). 'Ecosystem legitimacy emergence. A collective action view'. *Journal of Management*, **48**(3), 515–541.

Tippmann, E., Ambos, T.C., Del Giudice, M., Monaghan, S. and Ringov, D. (2023). 'Scale-ups and scaling in an international business context'. *Journal of World Business*, **58**(1), 101397.

Tripsas, M. and Gavetti, G. (2000). 'Capabilities, cognition and inertia: Evidence from digital imaging'. *Strategic Management Journal*, **21**(10/11), 1147–1161.

US Bureau of Labor Statistics (2024). *Establishment age and survival data*. Retrieved from https://www.bls.gov/bdm/us_age_naics_00_table7.txt (Last access: November 4, 2024).

Vergne, J.-P. and Durand, R. (2010). 'The missing link between the theory and empirics of path dependence: Conceptual clarification, testability issue, and methodological implications'. *Journal of Management Studies*, **47**(4), 736–759.

Vergne, J.-P. and Durand, R. (2011). 'The path of most persistence: An evolutionary perspective on path dependence and dynamic capabilities'. *Organization Studies*, **32**(3), 365–382.

Wholey, D.R. and Brittain, J.W. (1986), 'Organizational ecology: Findings and implications'. *Academy of Management Review*, **11**(3), 513–533.

Wievel, W. and Hunter, A. (1985). 'The inter-organizational network as a resource: A comparative case study on organizational genesis'. *Administrative Science Quarterly*, **30**(4), 482–496.

Yang, T. and Triana, M. (2019). 'Set up to fail: Explaining when women-led businesses are more likely to fail'. *Journal of Management*, **45**(3), 926–954.

Zaheer, S. (1995). 'Overcoming the liability of foreignness'. *Academy of Management Journal*, **38**(2), 341–363.

Zankl, J. and Grimes, M. (2024). 'Taming Unicorns: Toward a new normal of responsible entrepreneurship'. *Academy of Management Review*, **49**(4), 879–905.

Zollo, M. and Winter, S. (2002). 'Deliberate learning and the evolution of dynamic capabilities'. *Organization Science*, **13**(3), 339–351.

3 Enterprise failure and exit

3.1 Introduction

Why do enterprises fail? More specifically, why, when, and how do corporate crises happen? Addressing these questions has always been central in the research and practice about enterprise evolution and survival.

A strategic management perspective with which I am very much in line takes a middle ground between those scholars arguing that corporate crises are primarily the result of internal mistakes carried out at the governance and/or management level (e.g., Evergrande), and those scholars advancing that crises almost totally driven by external, environmental variables (e.g., COVID-19) are also possible. A key component of this perspective is understanding how the internal and external variables *co-evolve* (see Chapter 1, pp. 12–16); to do this, focusing on the "upper echelons" of a company (Hambrick and Mason, 1984) – and specifically on their misperceptions in decision-making – could help. As explained in Chapter 2 (pp. 34–35), misperceptions can be considered inappropriate assessments about the status (or dynamics) regarding either the internal or external variables (e.g., Hammond et al., 1998). In this case, misperceptions can specifically serve as the linking pin between the two variables. Relatedly, the perspective also attributes importance to the so-called "triggering event" (Billings et al., 1980; Shrivastava et al., 1988), i.e., an extraordinary, isolated event of internal or external nature, which has the *power* to transform a corporate situation of decline into that of a formal crisis needing urgent interventions to avoid failure (McKinley et al., 2014). Recently, for example, COVID-19 can be considered as that triggering event which has definitely caused a number of already pre-existing cases of corporate decline evolving into final bankruptcy.

On this premise, this chapter seeks to illustrate how different, intertwined streams of research around corporate crises have flourished over time and what support these streams have offered to the progress of the enterprise evolution research field. In this regard, the structure of this chapter is as follows. First, the chapter adopts a strategic management perspective to address the

DOI: 10.4324/9781003412663-3

"why" question, i.e., it provides its readers with an initial conceptualization of a corporate crisis and of its possible determinants. Second, this chapter addresses the "when" question, i.e., it provides an overview of the potential time dynamics regarding crises' development. Third, this chapter addresses the "how" question, highlighting the main classifications and typologies of corporate crises provided by the strategic management literature over time. Fourth, this chapter offers a focus on the role of human resources in general, and of top management teams in particular, when corporate crises are concerned. Summary and takeaways for scholars, practitioners, and students conclude this chapter.

3.2 Corporate crises. Why?

When we consider enterprises as the unit of analysis, we can argue that, over time, two intertwined streams of research on corporate crises have mainly progressed in parallel. The former, which does not constitute object of focus in this chapter, includes those studies embracing a financial perspective and committed to develop appropriate models to predict the insolvency of companies (e.g., Altman, 1968). The latter, which instead constitutes the core of this chapter, is the strategic management perspective, including those studies seeking to understand the determinants and time-related aspects of crises (e.g., Argenti, 1976; Smart and Vertinsky, 1977).

In general, from the strategic management perspective, an enterprise is said "to be in crisis" when it is perceived to face the real possibility to be *selected out* from its competitive landscape, which means to fail. In particular, and especially, if we consider what is explained in Chapter 1 (pp. 5–12), from this perspective a corporate crisis can be conceptualized as "deterioration in an organization's adaptation to its microniche and the associated reduction of resources within the organization" (Cameron et al., 1988: 9). With their main profitability indicators increasingly poor (e.g., growing decrease of financial assets, continuous negative income, enduring loss of market shares), to avoid failure those enterprises suffering a crisis need, as soon as possible, to plan and execute effective and efficient "turnaround" (also known as "restructuring") strategies (e.g., Trahms et al., 2013). Relatedly, corporate turnarounds are often accompanied by the adoption of legal measures, such as Chapter 11 of the American Bankruptcy Code in the US (see Box 3.1), to contrast bankruptcy when there is the opportunity (e.g., Lee et al., 2011) or to rationalize the selling of corporate assets when avoiding failure is not possible (Adriaanse and van der Rest, 2017). In principle, a successful turnaround is said to have occurred when a company is able to return to normality, from an organizational, economic, and financial point of view (Bibeault, 2017).

Box 3.1 The rise and fall of the Enron Corporation: A timeline

- Enron (Houston, Texas) started its business in 1985 through merging the activities of Houston Natural Gas and Nebraska InterNorth.
- In the nineties, Enron was composed of four Strategic Business Units: Transportation & Distribution, Wholesale Services, Retail Energy Services, and International Projects.
- Enron's business was mainly focused on:

  1 Natural gas delivering within the US;
  2 Electricity production and distribution within the US;
  3 Energy commodities' financial trading.

- Enron rapidly changes its core business from hard assets (i.e., energy production and distribution) to soft assets (i.e., energy commodity financial derivatives' trade).
- In 1999, Enrononline was launched.
- In the years between 1998 and 2000, the firm's revenues increase from $31,26 billion to $100,789 billion (Annual Report, 2000). The soft assets increase from 26.8% to 61.1% of the overall Enron's assets.
- In 2000, Enron was the seventh most admired company according to Fortune's AMAC annual publication.
- In March 2001, a *Fortune* article raised some doubts on what kind of financial situation can really lay behind Enron's excellent reputation. SEC judiciary inquiries follow.
- In December, Enron's board admitted that Enron was covered of debts which it had previously hidden. Both private and institutional investors withdrew. Enron's stock evaluation deteriorated.
- On December 2, 2001, Enron filed for the Chapter 11 procedure. Its stock value had reached a peak of $90 per share in July. It is now $0.26 per share worth.

Source: Adapted from Cafferata and Abatecola (2017: 93–94).

On this premise, when it comes to the question of *why corporate crises occur*, from the beginning a first, although (as we have anticipated) not conclusive, a distinction can be made between "external" and "internal" crises:

- "external" crises are those which, when enterprises are concerned, one could primarily ascribe to environmental determinants, both at macro-economic and/or industrial levels. In this regard, for example, some famous historical examples can seem useful to offer insightful evidence. At the beginning of the 21st century, a huge, global recession (which is a macro-economic event) follows the September, 11 terrorist attack in the US. As a consequence of this, a number of companies in different industries are negatively affected at the individual level and suffer crises. If we again consider macro-economic events, a very similar determinant of this *cause-effect* relationship can be, more recently, individuated, in the COVID-19 pandemic. Likewise, more or less in the same period, the increasing lack of semi-conductors (which is an industrial event) causes serious performance problems, at the firm level, to companies in different businesses, such as automobiles and electronics;

- "internal" crises, conversely, are those which one could primarily ascribe to problems deriving, at the enterprise level, from inappropriate actions in terms of strategy, management, and/or operations. For example, if one looks at the automobile industry, at the end of the 1980s, Europe saw the substantive change from the "first motorization" market, featured by most of the demand searching for a car to buy for the first time, to the "substitution" market, instead featured by most of the demand already having one "first" car; associated with the latter market is thus the customers' search for a "second" (or even "third") car to accomplish specific needs (e.g., citycar, sports car, SUV, etc.). The evidence of those years demonstrates that those European car producers which, from a strategic point of view, have not promptly reacted to (or even anticipated) this environmental demand change, have heavily suffered in terms of performance (Volpato, 2009).

The above introduced, if we consider, for example, the second half of the 20th century, from a historical point of view three major types of evidence have progressively become manifest: (i) the focus on internal corporate crises (which starts in the 1970s) has preceded that on external crises (which starts in the 1980s); (ii) over time, the consideration, in terms of perceived frequency of occurrence, of corporate crises has changed. While, at the beginning, corporate crises have been prospected as unusual, rare events in the enterprise life cycle, they have later turned to be considered as physiological, expectable components of the socio-economic environment at the international level;[1] (iii) over time, strategic management scholars have converged in arguing that clustering corporate crises as *purely* external, or *purely* internal, is neither conceptually nor methodologically appropriate. Corporate crises mostly appear as the ultimate consequence of a joint mix of external and internal determinants running in parallel or in sequence (e.g., Mellahi and Wilkinson, 2004; Abatecola, 2007, 2012).

As a consequence of the above, it has also become seemingly clear that, when each case of corporate crisis is observed individually: (i) the composition of the determinants' mix can be different; (ii) capturing the impact of each single determinant on the overall crisis effect can be difficult. In this last regard, the possibility to attribute specific responsibilities to executives and managers has been demonstrated to be particularly problematic over time (see Box 3.2), also because of the particular difficulty experienced, in many cases, to collect appropriate data.

Box 3.2 The Enron collapse: Actors and actions

(Main) Actors	*Actions: Aggressive Accounting*
1. Enron's executives	1. Energy contracts
2. Auditing firms	2. Special Purpose Entities (SPEs)
3. Financial analysts	3. Related Party Transactions
4. Formal independent directors of Enron's board	4. Stock Options

How did *Enron* happen?

- Managerial greed, *macho culture*, and corporate strategic orientation towards short-term goals.
- Strategic planning supported through manipulating the accounting books: *Enron is not what it seems.*

Consequences

- After the discovery of the Enron fraud in 2001, 2002 is the year which definitely represents the "season" of the financial scandals in the US, with various *Too Big to Fail* giants of corporate America as the main protagonists. A leader in the telecommunication industry worldwide, Worldcom constitutes one of the largest bankruptcies ever in the US, accompanied by the cases of Global Crossing (optical fibres), Qwest and Dynegy (energy), Adelphia Communication (cable television), and Xerox (printing). Likewise, Europe is also affected. In Italy, for example, the sadly famous cases of Cirio and Parmalat soon came to light.
- To combat financial frauds, several corporate governance reforms have been undertaken over the past (e.g., Sarbanes-Oxley Act in the US) and recent (e.g., Dodd-Frank Act) years. However, much has still seemingly to be done, not only from a research point of view (e.g., Troisi et al., 2022; Cucari et al., 2023) but also from a practical policymaking perspective (e.g., Zattoni and Cuomo, 2008; Gnan et al., 2013).

Source: Adapted from Cafferata and Abatecola (2017: 95–97).

This is also why the research methods adopted to study the topic have been various, ranging from quantitative to qualitative analyses (e.g., Bundy et al., 2017; Abatecola, 2019).

3.3 Corporate crises. When?

According to the strategic management perspective, a corporate crisis is, as we have explained, the result, in most of the cases, of the joint action of external (i.e., environment-related) and internal (i.e., firm-specific) factors, with every single case of crisis constituting a good storytelling material for scholars, business school students, and policymakers.

On this premise, we have already introduced that, in principle, the status of corporate crisis is generally associated with the necessity of corrective actions which are both urgent and substantive (Slatter, 1984). If these actions are not promptly put in place, distressed enterprises are ineluctably destined to fail. It is also clear that the nature of these actions can vary according to the case and their accurate planning needs careful thinking at the top decision-making level. For example, if we recall a famous work by Robert Billings, Thomas Milburn, and Mary Lou Schaalman (1980), the analysis of a corporate crisis can stimulate three different behavioural approaches, i.e., "inaction", "routine" solutions, and "original/non-routine" solutions (pp. 304–305):

i "inaction" ("Are the risks serious if I don't change?" [p. 305]). This approach substantially builds on the belief that a specific crisis situation can be destined to end by itself and, thus, that no specific corrective actions need to be taken. It is clear that this approach not only can appear thought provocative, but also, from more than one aspect, considerably risky. When attempting to explain it, one of the business examples that I have recently used in the classroom regards the recent responses of traditional restaurants to COVID-19. Many *traditional* restaurants (i.e., with almost no food home delivery service) have suffered a crisis because of the lockdown associated with the pandemic. Relatedly, one key decision to enhance the restaurants' survival chances in the short term has been, in many cases, to cut the workforce to reduce costs. Indeed, once the lockdown has ended, new costs have been faced to rehire workforce. Thus, in terms of juxtaposing points of view, one point is from those who argue that the new costs faced have been ultimately higher than the previous costs saved. The other counterpoint, however, is from those who argue that, without the previous costs saved, during the lockdown many restaurants would have been forced to close (and many, nevertheless, have ultimately done so);

ii "routine" solutions ("If the answer exists in a book it is simply not a crisis" [p. 305]). This approach substantially builds on the belief that the crisis can be countervailed through a standardized organizational response. For example, the business world is full of stories in which one of the first actions executed to restructure distressed companies is that of replacing the Board of Directors in general, and the Chief Executive Officer in particular; however, as we also discuss later in this chapter, this is not necessarily an action which always *pays*. Relatedly, another action which appears as a recurring theme in the restructuring plans of distressed firms is that of cutting costs, especially if these costs are found to be associated with activities which, from Michael Porter's value chain perspective (1985), are not key. Finally, and especially in the case of well-known, important companies, one another often executed action almost always regards the adoption of an effective communication strategy to reassure both the shareholders and stakeholders that the crisis is *under control*. This is done because, especially when a crisis regards a key brand, it is often associated with the escalation of the media comment (e.g., Davies et al., 2003; Siano et al., 2017);

iii "original/non-routine" solutions. In this approach, the corporate top decision-makers believe that the inaction, or routine-based solutions explained above, cannot result in appropriate to solve the crisis; thus, new (and hardly standardisable) solutions have to be adopted. To understand this approach, an example from the crisis faced, at the beginning of this century, by the famous Italian car producer Fiat might help. One of the most important Italian companies ever, between the end of the 1990s and the beginning of the 2000s Fiat finds itself in the mid of one of its most preoccupying crises (e.g., Di Minin et al., 2010). In particular, the performance of its automobile core business continuously decreases because of both external (e.g., competition increase) and internal (e.g., reduced competitiveness of the car portfolio) determinants; in contrast, the performance of (at least) some among its other businesses (Fiat is a relatedly diversified group) remains stable, when not positive. This considered, if using the routine-based approach explained above, Fiat could downsize the (negatively performing) core business to cut costs and, in parallel, could continue to reinforce the (positively performing) other businesses. Indeed, Fiat substantially does the contrary; this means that, for example, it sells some positively performing businesses and refocuses on the core business by reinvesting the revenues from the selling. As the main explanation of this, Fiat's historical founding family firmly believes that the group would almost totally lose its DNA without its centenary automobile brand, for which it has become known and largely appreciated worldwide (e.g., Volpato, 2009).

The above explained, when it (even more specifically) comes to the question of *when corporate crises happen*, over time the explanatory models developed by scholars have been undoubtedly flourishing. In general, and again according to Billings et al. (1980), the cases of corporate crisis occurring all of a sudden have been considered, indeed, rare. On the contrary, crisis situations have been mostly conceived only as the ultimate consequence of the gradual, although continuous deterioration of the enterprise performance over time. In parallel, there is no doubt that, when exploding and becoming clear to all the corporate shareholders and stakeholders, the impact of a crisis assumes a "global" posture; this posture urgently calls into action the evaluation about a company's survival chances (e.g., Dewaelheyns et al., 2017), with the *hard* choice between turnaround and closing (De Ruysscher, 2017).

In particular, a landmark crisis modelization by Thomas Milburn, Randall Schuler, and Kenneth Watman (1983) comprises three key moments following one another: "antecedents", which can be externally and/or internally related; "moderators", both of the antecedents and of their relationships; "strategic responses", both at an individual and organizational level. Likewise, Paul Shrivastava, Ian Mitroff, Danny Miller, and Anne Miglani (1988: 297) argue that crises "have fundamental trans-national causes, involving social, political and cultural variables". Crises are thus composed of "loosely coupled" events, where "each event sets the stage for others to occur in a chain reaction that proliferates the crisis" (p. 292). Relatedly, and as already prospected by Billings et al. (1980), according to Shrivastava et al. (1988: 288) the most acute phase of a crisis is catalyzed by the occurrence of a specific "triggering event", conceivable as an identifiable event which can be potentially isolated over time and space. In this regard, for example:

i *Bhopal crisis*: this case regards the Union Carbide (I) Ltd. plant in the crowded city of Bophal (India). In the 1980s, this plant produced a large quantity of the highly poisonous chemical Methyl Isocyanate (MIC), used as a key input to produce the pesticide SEVIN. On December 2, 1984, because of an inappropriate pipe-washing operation, a large quantity of water entered in contact with MIC, with large quantities of the latter released into the atmosphere. As a consequence, about 3,000 people died and 300,000 were severely injured. In this regard, what needs to be highlighted is that, since its commissioning in 1981, the plan has continuously received inappropriate maintenance. Thus, from a conceptual point of view, the pipe-washing operation only acts as the triggering event of the crisis, which seems to have its primary antecedents in the poor plant ordinary management (Shrivastava, 1992);
ii *Challenger disaster*: this case regards the explosion, on January 28, 1986, of the Space Shuttle Challenger 74 seconds after its take-off from the NASA Space Center of Cape Canaveral (7 people die). The triggering event, also in this case, is the malfunctioning of the right-side solid rocket booster powering the shuttle. Indeed, however, several primary antecedents are later identified by the US judicial inquiries (e.g., Rogers

et al., 1986), including inappropriate manufacturing of some shuttle components, ineffective risk management, internal communication gaps, etc.[2]

When the time dynamics of a corporate crisis are concerned, what we have highlighted so far is, more generally, also in line with the well-known strategic management theories regarding shareholder value creation (Fruhan, 1979; Rappaport, 1986). In fact, stemming from those theories, a number of scholars have given significant attention not only to crisis but also to "decline" situations. A phase of the firm's life cycle in which the crisis is still somehow hidden, the concept of decline needs to be intended as a continuously negative performance, over time, in terms of loss of corporate value (e.g., D'Aveni, 1989; Van Witteeloostuijn, 1998). In its potentially subsequent progress, if degraded by a triggering event internal or external to the enterprise, the decline can ultimately evolve into a crisis status (e.g., Hambrick and D'Aveni, 1988; Weitzel and Johnson, 1989).

3.4 Corporate crises. How?

What we have explained above could be summarized through the words of Mitroff, according to whom

> "[…] organizations do create themselves the crisis they face in the sense that the kind of early warning, prevention, damage limitation, recovery and learning mechanism they institute is one of the most important factors affecting what kind of crisis occurs".
>
> (1988: 19)

Ultimately, corporate crises can be considered as moments of serious instability, in which relevant economic losses can produce the following financial pressures: (i) loss of trust and credit capacity, (ii) cash flow insolvency, and (iii) stock value collapse (with i, ii, and iii – often – sequentially occurring).

In principle, the financial pressures above almost always raise the urgency of new external funding or (at least) of extensions to that existing (i.e., debt renegotiation). In this regard, it is clear that additional funding (in terms of volume and/or time) results possible only when (at least) two conditions are contemporaneously satisfied: (i) the corporate governance of a distressed firm is, in general, perceived as reliable and capable to restructure the enterprise (e.g., Hambrick and D'Aveni, 1992); (ii) this governance is also able to appropriately communicate its intended restructuring plan (e.g., D'Aveni and MacMillan, 1990). When these two conditions are not met, the opening of insolvency/bankruptcy procedures becomes unavoidable. For example, this is what, among others, has seemingly differentiated the destiny of General Motors and Enron in the US at the beginning of this century. Both these corporations suffered a crisis, but only the former met favourable support, in terms of new funding, by the external environment, which means the US government in this case.

In sum, from a strategic management perspective, a corporate crisis often appears as the last and most dramatic evolution of the decline phase; during the crisis, all the economic and financial disequilibria become totally manifest.[3] As a consequence, market trust often erodes and failure can be avoided only when significant interventions of industrial and financial restructuring are promptly planned and successfully executed. Relatedly, when it (even) more specifically comes to the question of *how corporate crises happen*, further considerations can be elicited if we go back to the anticipated distinction between the external and internal determinants of a crisis. As for the former, for example, we have written that external determinants can have a macro-economic and/or industrial nature. To explain more, we can add here that, (at least) because among the most frequent, the following determinants have historically appeared to be worth of mention: (a) underdevelopment of some financial markets, especially in terms of support to firms' listing and market capitalization; (b) inefficiency of some banking systems, with particular regard to the high interest rates payed to obtain credit; (c) instability of the money exchange rate systems, that can have a major impact especially on those companies in which exports are a key contributor to the overall revenues; (d) underdevelopment of primary infrastructures, such as the transport and telecommunication systems (as for the latter, for example, one might think about the so-called "Digital Divide"); (e) political tensions and/or environmental disasters (we could simply count how heavily the international stock markets daily decrease when a new conflict starts, or when a calamity takes place); and (f) poor quality of the corporate governance systems, especially in terms of rules to protect investors when corporate frauds are discovered (see again, for example, Boxes 3.1 and 3.2).

The above illustrated for the external determinants, the typological clusterings of internal determinants have been also many. In this regard, I have always found particularly explanatory a ground-breaking classification developed by Luigi Guatri (e.g., 1995), according to whom the main internal determinants of a corporate crisis can be substantially individuated, among others, in the following: (a) inefficiency; (b) overcapacity; (c) product obsolescence; and (d) strategic myopia. Table 3.1 presents their most distinctive features.

Related to the above, what can finally result also interesting (and, from more than one aspect, also thought-provocative) is the idea that corporate crises can be classified not only if we consider their possible determinants but also if we consider the reasons which, in a supposed crisis' situation, can obstacle a successful corporate turnaround (e.g., Schmitt and Raisch, 2013). In this regard, for example, I have always found particularly significant a pioneering classification proposed by Pellegrino Capaldo (1977), according to whom the typologies of a corporate crisis can be distinguished in (a) financial, (b) economic, and (c) economic-financial. Table 3.2 presents their most distinctive characteristics.

Table 3.1 Some significant internal determinants of a corporate crisis

Type	*Key Features*
Inefficiency	*Meaning*: Specific activities in the firm's value chain are not competitive because their contribution margin is not in line with their comparative average. In many cases, inefficiency primarily affects the production activity, where it can be specifically observed in terms of production costs or, more generally, of efficiency indicators. *Relationship with performance*: The industrial cost, at the single product level, is benchmarked to that of the main competitors. This benchmark can be insightful, especially when the degree of use of the plants' productive capacity is, in parallel, observed. In this regard, a moderate, or more significant, inefficiency, can emerge. The former can decrease if the use of the productive capacity increases; the consequence of the latter, instead, is that the average product cost is higher than that of the competitors, also when output volumes increase.[4] *Notes*: Not limited to production, inefficiency can also regard other business areas, such as administration, information systems, or financial management (e.g., budgeting, credit negotiation).
Overcapacity	*Meaning*: There is an excess of offering volumes regarding a good/service. Overcapacity often happens at the industry level, with the effect of generating an overall demand decrease for every firm in the industry (with the associated decrease of revenues). Antecedents of industrial overcapacity can be individuated, for example, in the obsessive search for scale economies, massive import volumes in a specific country and, perhaps even more importantly, in the decrease of a good/service demand deriving from a change in the customers' preferences. *Relationship with performance*: The impact of overcapacity on firms' performance depends on how they are able to adapt (see Chapter 1, pp. 5–12). While the more competitive firms are able to compensate the demand decrease through increasing their market shares, the less competitive firms witness a contemporaneous double decrease (i.e., demand and market shares). Especially in the latter case, the firms' capability to reduce costs (e.g., plants, structure, human resources) as soon as possible becomes key to enhance their survival chances. *Notes*: Sometimes overcapacity does not regard the industry, but only the firm level. In this case, it specifically depends on the demand reduction for the firm's goods/services because they have simply lost competitiveness. This situation appears particularly problematic because, among others, the environment is often reluctant to accept cuts to the workforce to reduce costs. In this case, in fact, it does not perceive the whole industry as suffering a crisis.

(Continued)

Table 3.1 (Continued)

Product obsolescence	*Meaning*: Obsolescence is a particular case of inefficiency (see also above) regarding the product mix offer, with negative consequences on the firm's market shares and performance. Its antecedents can regard the industry, such as cyclical fluctuations,[5] or the firm, such as lack of innovation associated with the product life cycle. Not limited to the features of a product, obsolescence can also regard the marketing strategies associated with it, such as promotion, choice of customers' targets, services offered and/or, more in general, corporate image. *Relationship with performance*: Risk definitely seems to be higher in mono-product firms because product margins appear physiologically less likely to be compensated. This is also the reason why, at a certain point, many firms choose to diversify their business. *Notes*: Product mix and marketing choices, as obsolescence determinants, are often intertwined. On the one hand, when its quality decreases, the product mix reduces margins and, thus, also the space for new marketing investments; on the other hand, the need to recover market share increases the possibility of marketing mistakes.
Strategic myopia	*Meaning*: In this situation, firms appear to pay more attention to short-term goals than to long-term sustainable performance. *Relationship with performance*: Almost all the firms suffering decline or crisis show a lack of strategic planning, presenting irrational plans which are also associated with scarce stakeholders' engagement. *Notes*: The causal relationship between lack of strategic planning and crisis does not always occur; the contrary, sometimes, can happen, with the crisis itself as the main cause of the lack of corporate strategic planning.

Source: Adapted from Guatri (1995: 117–145).

As a final consideration to what explained so far, it seems clear that the most vivid common feature between the typologies illustrated in Tables 3.1 and 3.2 is still (and almost always) the role played by human resources (e.g., Morrow et al., 2007; Fortune and Mitchell, 2012).

3.5 Executives, decision-making, and corporate crises

As seminally stated by Isadore Barmash (1973: 299): "Corporations are managed by men; and men, never forget, manage organizations to suit themselves. Thus corporate calamities are calamities created by men". As also illustrated above, when human resources are concerned, one general statement by strategic management scholars has been that corporate crises are, more than often,

Table 3.2 Financial, economic, and economic-financial crises

Type	*Meaning*
Financial	These crises can be considered as situations in which a firm does not have, and is not able to supply, the financial resources appropriate to safely conduct its daily business. If observed from a strict economic perspective, however, its business could be considered in equilibrium.
Economic	These crises mostly derive from unfavourable scenarios associated with the demand of the firms' goods/services, together with the cost of their production. This typology, in other words, presents many similarities with the inefficiency, overcapacity, product obsolescence or strategic myopia typologies illustrated in Table 3.1.
Economic-financial	More unusual than the two above, this typology of crises regards those specific cases in which, on the one hand, a firm does not appear able to sustain the financial distress deriving from a previous economic crisis which it has suffered. On the other hand, however, if we do not consider the current financial distress, from a strict economic perspective the firm's business could be considered in equilibrium.

Source: Adapted from Capaldo (1977: 316–320).

the result of ineffective and inefficient strategic planning (and/or execution) at the top decision-making level (e.g., Wiesenfeld et al., 2008; Grant, 2024). In this regard, for example, according to a pioneering synthesis by Guatri (1995: 114–115) drawing on previous evidence from the US (Bibeault, 1982), the following three organizational contexts, among others, should raise warning signals when present:

a *monocracy*: a first, possible antecedent for the crisis of an enterprise is associated with the circumstance in which one single person is individually responsible for the firm's management. This circumstance does not only occur in small firms because it is associated with an entrepreneurial phase including, almost always, also the medium and large firms attempting to implement (or continue) a growth process. In many cases, however, monocratic management *de facto* results substantially inappropriate with the increase of environmental dynamism (e.g., McCarthy et al., 2010) and, as a consequence, of management complexity (e.g., Surace, 2019). A more structured management seems thus necessary to support long-term survival;

b *weak management*: management is entrusted to persons whose skills result only partially in line with those requested to conduct managerial roles. This circumstance can be the consequence of monocracy (see above), in which the "boss" does not want influential persons around her/him (e.g., Sutton, 2010), or it can simply be the consequence of poor choices regarding the selection of human resources;

c *underdeveloped monitoring of the Board of Directors:* as the past and most recent cases of financial fraud show (see, again, for example, Boxes 3.1 and 3.2), the Boards' actions have often lacked careful scrutiny by external bodies. Major corporate problems, as a consequence, can arise, especially when hubris, greed, and ego result as key characteristics of some executives (e.g., Picone et al., 2014).

On this premise, and as we have also introduced at the beginning of this chapter, scholars argue that managerial actions are substantially guided by those perceptions which managers intrinsically own and develop over time (e.g., Bowden, 2017), with regard both to their firm and its external environment (e.g., Adinolfi, 2021; Secchi and Cowley, 2021). When these perceptions are wrong (e.g., Randolph-Seng, 2009; Acciarini et al., 2021), crises can occur. In this regard, the potential relationship between a corporate crisis and the configuration of its top management team seemingly merits specific attention, especially with regard to the team's composition and tenure (e.g., Mellahi and Wilkinson, 2004; Abatecola et al., 2014). In particular, as far as composition is concerned, some studies have evidenced that, especially in turbulent environments, heterogeneous teams are more successful than homogeneous teams in managing crisis situations (e.g., Minichilli and Hansen, 2007). From a psychological point of view (Mellahi and Wilkinson, 2004), well-known reasonings against homogeneity have been, for example, the negative influence of "groupthink" on individual decision-making (Janis, 1972); or, the negative tendency towards "rigidity" in decision-making, when in front of environmental threats, to protect the *status quo* (Staw et al., 1981). In principle, however, one could also argue that, during a crisis, having a homogeneous top management team not necessarily is totally harmful. In fact, we can consider that, in the particular situation of a crisis, the decision-making speed often results among those factors which are key to improve the survival chances of a company. In this regard, we also know that, in general, homogeneous teams tend to decide more rapidly than heterogeneous teams.

Likewise, as far as tenure is concerned, in the mid of a crisis long-tenured teams seemingly tend to underestimate the situation, or (at least) to consider external, more than internal, determinants as the primary antecedents of the crisis. Again from a psychological point of view (Mellahi and Wilkinson, 2004), the main reason for this behaviour would stand in the well-known concept of "denial" (e.g., Brown and Starkey, 2000), which means the substantial refusal to acknowledge a potentially critical situation. In some cases, denial can derive from subjective difficulties in terms of learning, related, for example, to positive past performance (e.g., Miller, 1990), with associated self-reinforcing and path dependence mechanisms occurring (see also Chapter 2, pp. 33–35). In other cases, however, denial can happen because top decision-makers consciously want to avoid admitting personal responsibilities with regard to strategic decisions, which have proven inappropriate *ex post*. When corporate performance is concerned, denial can be dramatic. In this regard, for example, a case study about the crisis faced by the famous UK retailer Marks and Spencer at the end of the 20th century has been particularly illustrative (Mellahi et al., 2002). This case study shows that the company managers *denied* the reliability of the customers' feedbacks, raising doubts about the data validity. In other words, the managers denied the company problems highlighted in the feedbacks, until the corporate crisis harshly exploded.

The above introduced with regard to tenure, if we (even) more specifically question whether the changing of the top management team can be itself considered as a crisis antecedent, research has shown contradictory evidence. Relatedly, as we know, changing the top management team often results as one of the first consequences of a corporate crisis (e.g., Lohrke et al., 2004; Wiesenfeld et al., 2008), especially when poor management is perceived to be one of its primary determinants. However, is this change always beneficial? As also anticipated before in this chapter (p. 49), the answer to this question is not necessarily "yes". For example, a ground-breaking study by Gordon Donaldson (1994) supports the idea that a successful corporate turnaround can also be internally conjectured and implemented. This study explores the strategic reasons, in the 1980s, that led some American market-leading firms of the 1970s and 1980s (e.g., General Mills, Burlington Northern e CPC International) to suffer significant crises. This study then shows that these firms are able to execute radical and effective corporate restructuring through a totally internal rethinking process; they redefine missions, goals, strategy, and structure without the necessity of external intervention. From the study, Donaldson puts forward the idea that, in principle, internal corporate restructuring can be no less effective than one external, with the latter triggered, for example, by hostile takeovers. In fact, the former has sometimes the advantage to avoid the trauma associated with an external intervention, of which, for example, breaking down daily activities appears as one of the most frequent short-term consequences (e.g., Miralles et al., 2022). In other words, according to Donaldson, it is true that internal restructuring needs more time, than external turnaround, to be effective. However, it is also true that, if observed from a long-term perspective, internal restructuring shows higher and more complete potential of success.

Related to strategic planning, "growth traps" (i.e., the decision-making traps potentially associated with processes of intended strategic growth) can finally merit consideration. As we know, growing is per se risky (e.g., Kaplan and Mikes, 2012; Hristov et al., 2024), with planned growth strategies not necessarily translating, *de facto*, into competitive success. In the business world, we have not rarely experienced growth processes not rationally planned. Some of these processes, for example, can result too fast, because they are not aligned to the extant level of organizational assets; as a result, they often require massive leverage to be sustained, determining financial disequilibrium as a threat (e.g., Brunelli and Di Carlo, 2020; Cafferata, 2022: 310–316). At the same time (see, again, for example, Boxes 3.1 and 3.2), we have seen growth processes mostly set to pursue the personal interests of some executives rather than those of shareholders and stakeholders (e.g., Stoelhorst and Vishwanathan, 2024). In sum, there is always a component of uncertainty associated with growth. When implemented, on the one hand, growth can be revealed to be even more successful than what was planned, such as in the case of Unicorns;[6] but, on the other hand, it can also reveal to be more problematic, resulting (in some cases) even into a final corporate crisis. In this regard, the fallacy in strategic planning and/or execution often plays a key role (e.g., Lovallo et al., 2023). Examples have included (e.g., Guatri, 1995: 81–82): (a) poor forecasting about supposed demand trends for goods and services; (b) understatement of potential entry barriers in particular industries and/or geographical areas; (c) understatement of the potential limitations associated with the extant organizational structure; (d) lack of what Sheryl Sandberg and Adam Grant (2017) would more generally call an "Option-B", which – in our case – would mean lack of (at least) one sustainable alternative thought to be put in place in the case of failure of the growth plan.

The above explained, the pressure towards short-term performance is another specific threat associated with growth in general, and growth speed in particular, especially when firms operate in turbulent environments featured by hypercompetition (D'Aveni, 1994) and, often, also copycatting (Yu, 2018). In fact, in the case of extant limited resources, the initial profitability deriving from the growth process is often low, sometimes even absent; the reason here consists in the additional costs to be sustained for those new investments (especially in intangible assets such as marketing and R&D) necessary to grow. Indeed, risk can be embedded also in the opposite situation, i.e., in the case of abundance of extant resources. For example, especially to pursue a supposed higher reputation for the corporate executives, this abundance could support superfluous unrelated diversification strategies through M&As. The consequence could be not only a radical deviation from the initial goals of long-term sustainable performance but also poor short-term financial benefits and increased risk posture.

3.6 Summary

During their life cycle, enterprises almost always deal with physiological situations of performance instability. Not all these situations, however, ultimately shift into the status of a formal crisis, with this status requiring an appropriate, specific turnaround to avoid corporate failure (e.g., Adriaanse, 2017; Barbero et al., 2017). Supported by examples from the practice of business, in this chapter, we have adopted a strategic management perspective to explain the most significant conceptualizations (i.e., the "why", "when", and "how" questions) associated with corporate crises. Among those discussed, the main takeaways of the chapter could be thus summarized as follows.

First, from a conceptual point of view, we have explained a corporate crisis with a focus on its most negative aspects for an enterprise. Specifically, the strategic management literature conceptualizes a crisis as the most acute stage of a cumulated process, continuous over time, of inefficacies and inefficiencies regarding strategic planning and/or execution. If not properly combatted, this process causes the decrease of competitiveness for the enterprise, which then translates into a performance decline (e.g., Ndofor et al., 2013). Especially when amplified by the occurrence of an external or internal triggering event, decline ultimately translates into crisis.

Second, which also relates to research methods, we have explained that decline and crisis are mostly caused by the simultaneous occurrence of internal and external determinants, often overlapping over time. However, we have also noted that quantifying their weight in the final collapse is often a challenging task. When internal determinants are concerned, for example, it is clear that the firm's (increasing or decreasing) competitiveness does not depend only on its top management team. Qualified human resources, in terms of middle/lower level management and operations, always play a no less important role. Thus, especially when a corporate crisis devastates large firms, attributing specific responsibilities, at the human resource level, is rarely simple (Chapter 4 will elaborate on this point).

In conclusion, corporate crises continue to occur constantly in the business world. This is also why, if we want to increase the understanding of how crises can be countervailed (e.g., Konig et al., 2020) or (even better) prevented, research-based evidence on their antecedents and time dynamics continues to deserve permanent attention in the strategic management scholarly agenda. In this regard, and in line with the previous chapters of this book, the contribution of this chapter can be both conceptual and methodological. From a conceptual point of view, this chapter can help understand why (and how) a number of concepts related to enterprise failure and exit have been flourishing over time. At the same time, from a methodological point of view, this chapter can help understand what key elements need to be carefully considered when enterprises aim to plan (and execute) successful performance recovery.

Notes

1 This changing perception, by the strategic management scholars, around the frequency of corporate crises has run in parallel with the changing perception, by the

political economists, around the frequency of "industrial" crises (e.g., Galbraith, 1987). Considered as those affecting an industry – as a whole – in its entire value chain, the latter crises also substantially change the way in which they are perceived, i.e. from situational to permanent.

2 Together with plenty of others, the sadly famous narratives of Bophal and the Challenger have also constituted inputs for subsequent, well-known categorizations of corporate crises. For example, according to Thierry Pauchant and Ian Mitroff (1992), crises need to be clustered along two dimensions: origin (internal/external) and nature (human-social/technical-economic).

3 Developed over the years, the discipline known as "Crisis Management" is that aimed at planning and executing effective and efficient reactions to a crisis, especially when it is in its most acute phase (e.g., Mitroff and Pearson, 1993; Pearson and Clair, 1998). According to this discipline, preventing this acute phase also assumes a key role.

4 The benchmark can also regard the performance of the most relevant production factors, such as human resources, technological know-how, and procurement.

5 On the basis of precise governmental choices, antecedents, sometimes, can also be individuated in new import trends associated with heavily reduced prices.

6 Chapter 4 (pp. 70–71) will also expand on this point.

References

Abatecola, G. (2007). *Crisi d'impresa. Elementi di teoria e evidenze empiriche.* Aracne.

Abatecola, G. (2012). 'Interpreting corporate crises: Towards a co-evolutionary approach'. *Futures*, **44**(10), 860–869.

Abatecola, G. (2019). 'Reviewing corporate crises: A strategic management perspective'. *International Journal of Business and Management*, **14**(5), 21–31.

Abatecola, G., Farina, V. and Gordini, N. (2014). 'Board effectiveness in corporate crises. Lessons from the evolving empirical research'. *Corporate Governance: The International Journal of Business in Society*, **14**(4), 531–542.

Acciarini, C., Brunetta, F. and Boccardelli, P. (2021). 'Cognitive biases and decision-making strategies in times of change: A systematic literature review'. *Management Decision*, **59**(3), 638–652.

Adinolfi, P. (2021). 'A journey around decision-making: Searching for the "big picture" across disciplines'. *European Management Journal*, **39**(1), 9–21.

Adriaanse, J. (2017). 'Back to the future: The General Motors restructuring plan'. In J. Adriaanse and J.P. van der Rest (Eds.), *Turnaround management and bankruptcy*. Routledge, 365–387.

Adriaanse, J. and van der Rest, J.P. (Eds., 2017). *Turnaround management and bankruptcy*. Routledge.

Altman, R. (1968). 'Financial ratios. Discriminant analysis and the prediction of corporate bankruptcy'. *Journal of Finance*, **23**(4), 589–609.

Argenti, J. (1976). *Corporate collapse. The cause and symptoms*. McGraw-Hill.

Barbero, J.L., Di Pietro, F. and Chiang, C. (2017). 'A rush of blood to the head: Temporal dimensions of retrenchment, environment and turnaround performance'. *Long Range Planning,* **50**(6), 862–879.

Barmash, I. (Ed., 1973). *Great business disasters. Swindlers, bunglers and frauds in American industry.* Ballantine Books.

Bibeault, D.B. (1982). *Corporate turnaround. How managers turn losers into winners*. Mc-Graw Hill.

Bibeault, D.B. (2017). 'The history of corporate turnaround. Personal reflections'. In J. Adriaanse and J.P. van der Rest (Eds.), *Turnaround management and bankruptcy*. Routledge, 3–21.

Billings, R.S., Milburn, T.W. and Schaalman, M.L. (1980). 'A model of crisis perception: A theoretical and empirical analysis'. *Administrative Science Quarterly*, **25**(8), 300–316.

Bowden, B. (2017). 'An exploration into the relationship between management and market forces: The railroads of Australia and the American West, 1880–1900'. *Journal of Management History*, **23**(3), 297–314.

Brown, A.D. and Starkey, K. (2000). 'Organizational identity and organizational learning: A psychodynamic pespective'. *Academy of Management Review*, **25**(1), 102–120.

Brunelli, S. and Di Carlo, E. (Eds., 2020). *Accountability, ethics and sustainability of organizations. New theories, strategies and tools for survival and growth*. Springer.

Bundy, J., Pfarrer, M.D., Short, C.E. and Coombs, W.T. (2017). 'Crises and crisis management: Integration, interpretation, and research development'. *Journal of Management*, **43**(6), 1661–1692.

Cafferata, R. (2022). *Management in adattamento. Tra razionalità economica, evoluzione ed imperfezione dei sistemi* (3rd edition). Il Mulino.

Cafferata, R. and Abatecola, G. (2017). *Enterprise evolution. Teaching notes*. Texmat.

Cameron K.A., Sutton R.I. and Whetten, A.D. (Eds., 1988). *Readings in organizational* dec*line: Frameworks, research and prescriptions*. Ballinger.

Capaldo, P. (1977). 'Crisi d'impresa e suo risanamento'. *Banche e Banchieri*, **5**, 315–329.

Cucari, N., Esposito De Falco, S., Yamak, S. and Lee, B. (Eds., 2023). *Handbook of research methods for corporate governance*. Edward Elgar.

D'Aveni, R.A. (1989). 'The aftermath of organizational decline: A longitudinal study of the strategic and managerial characteristics of declining firms'. *Academy of Management Journal*, **32**(3), 577–605.

D'Aveni, R.A. (1994). *Hypercompetition. Managing the dynamics of strategic maneuvering*. Free Press.

D'Aveni, R.A. and MacMillan, I.C. (1990). 'Crisis and the content of managerial communications: A study of the focus of attention of top managers in surviving and failing firms'. *Administrative Science Quarterly*, **35**(4), 634–657.

Davies, G., Chun, R., da Silva, R. and Roper, S. (2003). *Corporate reputation and competitiveness*. Routledge.

De Ruysscher, D. (2017). 'Business rescue, turnaround management, and the legal regime of default and insolvency in Western history (late middle ages to present day)'. In J. Adriaanse and J.P. van der Rest (Eds.), *Turnaround management and bankruptcy*. Routledge, 22–42.

Dewaelheyns, N., De Prijcker, S. and Van Den Heuvel, K. (2017). 'Predicting business failure'. In J. Adriaanse and J.P. van der Rest (Eds.), *Turnaround management and bankruptcy*. Routledge, 66–45.

Di Minin, A., Frattini, F. and Piccaluga, A. (2010). 'Fiat: Open innovation in a downturn (1993–2003)'. *California Management Review*, **52**(3), 132–159.

Donaldson, G. (1994). *Corporate restructuring. Managing the process from within.* Harvard Business School Press.

Enron Corporation (2000). *Annual report.*

Fortune, A. and Mitchell, W. (2012). 'Unpacking firm exit at the firm and industry levels: The adaptation and selection of firm capabilities'. *Strategic Management Journal,* **33**(7), 794–819.

Fruhan, W.E. (1979). *Financial strategy: Studies in the creation, transfer and destruction of shareholder value.* Irwin.

Galbraith, J.K. (1987). *Economics in perspective: A critical history.* Princeton University Press.

Gnan, L., Hinna, A., Monteduro, F. and Scarozza, D. (2013). 'Corporate governance and management practices: Stakeholder involvement, quality and sustainability tools adoption: Evidences in local public utilities'. *Journal of Management and Governance*, **17**(4), 907–937.

Grant, R.M. (2024). *Contemporary strategy analysis* (12th edition). John Wiley & Sons.

Guatri, L. (1995). *Turnaround. Declino, crisi e ritorno al valore*. EGEA.

Hambrick, D.C. and D'Aveni, R.A. (1988). 'Large corporate failures as downward spirals'. *Administrative Science Quarterly,* **33**(1), 1–23.

Hambrick, D.C. and D'Aveni, R.A. (1992). 'Top team deterioration as part of the downward spiral of large corporate bankruptcies'. *Management Science*, **38**(10), 1445–1466.

Hambrick, D.C. and Mason, P.A. (1984). 'Upper echelons: The organization as a reflection of its top managers'. *Academy of Management Review*, **9**(2), 193–206.

Hammond, J.S. III, Keeney, R.L. and Raiffa, H. (1998). 'The hidden traps of decision making'. *Harvard Business Review*, **76**(5), 47–58.

Hristov, I., Camilli, R., Chirico, A. and Mechelli, A. (2024). 'The integration between enterprise risk management and performance management system: Managerial analysis and conceptual model to support strategic decision-making process'. *Production Planning and Control*, **35**(8), 842–855.

Janis, I.L. (1972). *Victims of groupthink: A psychological study of foreign-policy decisions and fiascoes*. Houghton Mifflin.

Kaplan, R.S. and Mikes, A. (2012). 'Managing risks: A new framework'. *Harvard Business Review*, **90**(6), 48–60.

Konig, A.S., Graf-Vlachy, L., Bundy, J.N. and Little, L. (2020). 'A blessing and a curse: How CEOs' empathy affects their management of organizational crises'. *Academy of Management Review*, **45**(1), 130–153.

Lee, S.H., Yamakawa, Y., Peng, M.V. and Barney, J.B. (2011). 'How do bankruptcy laws affect entrepreneurship development around the world?'. *Journal of Business Venturing,* **26**(5), 505–520.

Lohrke, F.T., Bedeian, A.G. and Palmer, T.B. (2004). 'The role of top management teams in formulating and implementing turnaround strategies: A review and research agenda'. *International Journal of Management Reviews*, **5–6**(2), 63–90.

Lovallo, D., Cristofaro, M. and Flyvbjerg, B. (2023). 'Governing large projects: A three-stage process to get it right'. *Academy of Management Perspectives*, **37**(2), 138–156.

McCarthy, I.P., Lawrence, T.B., Wixted, B. and Gordon, B. (2010). 'A multidimensional conceptualization of environmental velocity'. *Academy of Management Review*, **35**(4), 604–626.

McKinley, W., Latham, S. and Braun, M. (2014). 'Organizational decline and innovation: Turnarounds and downward spirals'. *Academy of Management Review*, **39**(1), 88–110.

Mellahi, K., Jackson, P. and Sparks, L. (2002). 'An exploratory study into failure in successful organizations: The case of Marks & Spencer'. *British Journal of Management*, **13**(1), 15–29.

Mellahi, K. and Wilkinson, A. (2004). 'Organizational failure: A critique of recent research and a proposed integrative framework'. *International Journal of Management Reviews*, **5–6**(1), 21–41.

Milburn, T.W., Schuler, R.S. and Watman, K.H. (1983). 'Organizational crisis. Part I: Definition and conceptualization'. *Human Relations*, **36**(12), 1161–1180.

Miller, D. (1990). *The Icarus paradox: How exceptional companies bring about their own downfall. New lessons in the dynamics of corporate success, decline, and renewal*. Harper Business.

Minichilli, A. and Hansen, C. (2007). 'The board advisory tasks in small firms and the event of crises'. *Journal of Management and Governance*, **11**(1), 5–22.

Miralles, M., Lee, B., Dörfler, V. and Stierand, M. (2022). 'Guest editorial: Investigating trauma: Methodological, emotional and ethical challenges for the qualitative researcher'. *Qualitative Research in Organizations and Management*, **17**(4), 397–405.

Mitroff, I.I. (1988). 'Crisis management: Cutting through the confusion'. *Sloan Management Review*, **29**(2), 15–20.

Mitroff, I.I. and Pearson, C.M. (1993). *Crisis management. Diagnostic guide for improving your organization crisis-preparedness*. Jossey-Bass.

Morrow, J.L., Sirmon, D.G., Hitt, M.A. and Holcomb, T.R. (2007). 'Creating value in the face of declining performance: Firm strategies and organizational recovery'. *Strategic Management Journal,* **28**(3), 271–283.

Ndofor, H.A., Vanevenhoven, J. and Barker, V.L. (2013). 'Software firm turnarounds in the 1990s: An analysis of reversing decline in a growing, dynamic industry'. *Strategic Management Journal,* **34**(9), 1123–1133.

Pauchant, T.C. and Mitroff, I.I. (1992). *Transforming the crisis-prone organization. Preventing individual, organizational and environmental tragedies*. Jossey-Bass.

Pearson, C. and Clair, J. (1998). 'Reframing crisis management'. *Academy of Management Review*, **23**(1), 59–76.

Picone, P.M., Dagnino, G.B. and Minà, A. (2014). 'The origin of failure: A multidimensional appraisal of the hubris hypothesis and proposed research agenda'. *Academy of Management Perspectives*, **28**(4), 447–468.

Porter, M.E. (1985). *Competitive advantage. Creating and sustaining superior performance*. Free Press.

Randolph-Seng, B. (2009). 'The (mis)management of agency: Conscious belief and nonconscious self-control'. *Behavioral and Brain Sciences*, **32**(6), 532–533.

Rappaport, A. (1986). *Creating shareholder value. The new standard for business performance*. Free Press.

Rogers, W. et al. (1986). *Report of the Presidential Commission on the space shuttle Challenger accident*. Washington DC.

Sandberg, S. and Grant, A. (2017). *Option B. Facing adversity, building resilience, and finding joy*. Penguin Random House.

Schmitt, A. and Raisch, S. (2013). 'Corporate turnarounds: The duality of retrenchment and recovery'. *Journal of Management Studies*, **50**(7), 1216–1244.

Secchi, D. and Cowley, S.J. (2021). 'Cognition in organisations: What it is and how it works'. *European Management Review*, **18**(2), 79–92.

Shrivastava, P. (1992). *Bophal: Anatomy of a crisis* (2nd edition). Paul Chapman.

Shrivastava, P., Mitroff, I.I., Miller, D. and Miglani, A. (1988). 'Understanding industrial crises'. *Journal of Management Studies*, **25**(4), 285–303.

Siano, A., Vollero, A., Conte, F. and Amabile, S. (2017). '*More than words*: Expanding the taxonomy of greenwashing after the Volkswagen scandal'. *Journal of Business Research*, **71**, 27–37.

Slatter, S. (1984). *Corporate recovery: A guide to turnaround management.* Penguin Books.

Smart, C. and Vertinsky, I. (1977). 'Design for crisis decision units'. *Administrative Science Quarterly*, **22**(4), 640–657.

Staw, B., Sandelands, L. and Dutton, J.E. (1981). 'Threat–rigidity cycles in organizational behavior: A multi-level analysis'. *Administrative Science Quarterly*, **26**(4), 501–524.

Stoelhorst, J.W. and Vishwanathan, P. (2024). 'A stakeholder theory of corporate governance'. *Academy of Management Review*, **49**(1), 107–134.

Surace, A. (2019). 'Complexity and leadership: The case of a military organization'. *International Journal of Organizational Analysis*, **27**(5), 1522–1541.

Sutton, R.I. (2010). *Good boss, bad boss. How to be the best ... and learn from the worst.* Business Plus.

Trahms, C.A., Achidi Ndofor, A. and Sirmon, D.G. (2013). 'Organizational decline and turnaround: A review and agenda for future research'. *Journal of Management*, **39**(5), 1277–1307.

Troisi, R., Di Nauta, P. and Piciocchi, P. (2022). 'Private corruption: An integrated organizational model'. *European Management Review*, **19**(3), 476–486.

Van Witteeloostuijn, A. (1998). 'Bridging behavioral and economic theories of decline: Organizational inertia, strategic competition, and chronic failure'. *Management Science*, **44**(4), 501–518.

Volpato, G. (2009). 'Fiat Group Automobiles - An Arabian phoenix in the international auto industry'. In M. Freyssenet (Ed.), *The second automobile revolution – Trajectories of the world carmakers in the 21st century.* Palgrave Macmillan, 287–308.

Weitzel, W. and Johnson, E. (1989). 'Decline in organizations: A literature integration and extension'. *Administrative Science Quarterly*, **34**(1), 91–109.

Wiesenfeld, B.M., Wurthmann, K. and Hambrick, D.C. (2008). 'The stigmatization and devaluation of elites associated with corporate failures – A process model'. *Academy of Management Review,* **33**(1), 231–251.

Yu, H. (2018). *Leap. How to thrive in a world where everything can be copied.* PublicAffairs.

Zattoni, A. and Cuomo, F. (2008). 'Why adopt codes of good governance? A comparison of institutional and efficiency perspectives'. *Corporate Governance: An International Review*, **16**(1), 1–15.

4 The *Businesstype* – From research to practice

4.1 Introduction

In a recent report entitled *Sleeping Beauties*, (also) Clarivate argues that "older research present fresh opportunities to advance scientific and scholarly research today" (2024: 1). Among the different, famous examples mentioned in the report, "Albert Einstein predicted the existence of gravitational waves in 1916, a theory that was confirmed in 2015 by LIGO researchers" (p. 2). As explained in the report, "sleeping beauties" can be considered as those pieces of research which demonstrate impact only years (sometimes even decades) after their publication.

On this premise, the previous chapters of this book have attempted to explain how the literature about enterprise evolution has contributed to the strategic management domain by studying various phenomena associated with the enterprise life cycle, with a particular focus on the specific challenges of selective adaptation and environmental fit. It seems clear that many *classical* constructs and concepts discussed in the previous chapters cannot be considered as "sleeping beauties" because, as the chapters have illustrated, their impact on research and practice has been often profound from the very beginning. Surely, at the same time, it seems also clear that these constructs and concepts resonate with the spirit that "yesterday's findings fuel today's research breakthrough" (Clarivate, 2024: 1). Thus, it is mostly in this spirit that this chapter aims at providing its readers with further food for thought, in that it initially offers some potential avenues for future research in each of the areas considered so far. In fact, in terms of structure, the chapter first deals with enterprise evolution as a field, second with enterprise early survival (or mortality), and third with enterprise failure and exit. Fourth (and for each area), this chapter ends by also proposing some "how to" implications for managers, entrepreneurs, and policymakers. Summary and takeaways for scholars, practitioners, and students conclude this chapter.

DOI: 10.4324/9781003412663-4

4.2 Enterprise evolution

In a pioneering article published in the *Harvard Business Review*, Theodore Levitt (1965) conjectures the possible life cycle of a product as conceptually composed of four sequential phases: (i) introduction; (ii) growth; (iii) maturity, and (iv) decline. When explaining Levitt's model in the classroom, I always tell students that, especially if they aim to work (at least) in the marketing and/or R&D areas of a company, this model still represents a key piece of knowledge to be acquired and used. The model, for example, can help forecast how much each of the phases will be supposed to last; the model, at the same time, can help address the question of how a manager should deal with each of these phases (Cafferata and Abatecola, 2017: 63–67).

From the model, what (among others) can be particularly useful is how to cope with the product's maturity phase, where a problem of market saturation emerges. In this phase, as Levitt suggests through making the example of nylon, managers can plan specific actions to *extend* the product life cycle. These actions, for instance, can include promoting the use of the same product in new geographical areas or even promoting new uses for the same product. About the former action, for example, we could remember the international strategy adopted by the famous Italian car maker Fiat in the second half of the 1990s; with the European car industry witnessing its maturity stage, the firm attempts to enter Latin America by replicating many car models which, substantially, had already filled the absorptive capacity of Europe (Volpato, 2009). About the latter action, in parallel, the example regarding the evolution of the use of compact discs can be insightful; when introduced in the 1980s, compact discs were primarily utilized as high-quality devices (if compared to tapes) to listen to music. Later on, however, the development of streaming and digital platforms to listen to music progressively forces this use to change; the compact discs' life cycle is thus extended, as we know, by primarily proposing them as high-quality mass storage devices.[1]

The reason why Levitt's model has been used to open this section is that, we believe, it presents many visible and invisible colleges with a number of concepts developed in Chapter 1 of this book and on which this section aims to further expand. In fact, as I also stress in the classroom, although Levitt does consider the life cycle of products (and not of enterprises), his ideas have undoubtedly inspired many models of enterprise evolution subsequently developed (see again, for example, Chapter 1, p. 5). In this regard, as noted in the introduction to a well-regarded *Business Horizons* article by Roger Bennett and Robert Cooper (1984: 1),

> "many of the America's most successful companies have gone through a life cycle similar to the product life cycle. They began as innovators, and then grew to be giants in their markets. But, as their products mature, they need new products to continue company's growth".

In other words, especially if we consider the actions to extend the product life cycle illustrated above, the resulting idea is that successful firms are those able to adopt an *active* – and not only *reactive* – posture towards their external environment. Relatedly, as also highlighted by Robert Ayres and Wilbur Steger (1985: 66), "traditionally, it has been thought that a product life cycle is as irreversible as biological life cycle. That is, a product inevitably moves from birth to adolescence, maturity and death". However, "now there is mounting evidence that a turnabout in management thinking is under way. The new thinking is that it is actually possible to reverse the product life cycle" (p. 66).

All these considerations also resonate with the main takeaways emerging from Chapter 1. In particular, drawing on natural sciences – and on examples from the practice of business as well – Chapter 1 has offered a picture of how the enterprise evolution research field has developed over time. After having attempted to conceptually trace its boundaries, this chapter has first explained the long-standing dichotomy between environmental determinism and strategic voluntarism in shaping the adaptation and evolution of enterprises. This chapter has then explained how the dialectical and (later) co-evolutionary perspectives have substantially eliminated this dichotomy (e.g., Paniccia and Leoni, 2019). As we put forward below, adaptation on the one hand, and co-evolution on the other, can also merit some additional food for thought here.

First, which is also related to Levitt's trajectories for the product life cycle, we might question whether technological innovation is adaptation or, indeed, "exaptation" driven. In parallel with biological adaptation, the concept of exaptation also owes its theoretical roots within the field of natural sciences. Stephen Jay Gould and Elisabeth Vrba (1982) pioneeringly introduced exaptation as the set of all those organic characteristics that have been *co-opted* to their present use, although they had not been initially planned for it (in this regard, the example of the compact discs made above can be illustrative). In the 21st century, an increasing corpus of scholarly works has used the biological roots of exaptation to address the question of what drivers can really push forward radical technological innovation (e.g., Garud et al., 2016; Andriani and Kaminska, 2021). Nonetheless, this interesting research avenue seemingly needs further conceptual and methodological development. In particular, when enterprises are considered, the question of whether exaptation is serendipitous or not remains lively (e.g., Cattani and Mastrogiorgio, 2021; Simone et al., 2021). Relatedly, understanding the collective impact of exaptation mechanisms on the overall adaptation of enterprises also seemingly merits further empirical support (e.g., Dew and Sarasvathy, 2016).

Second, when adaptation is again considered, one of the themes that, in the strategic management literature, has been discussed a bit less is understanding how the adaptation process works when firms, indeed, do not change, i.e., they do not take any action. In other words, how can this process be explicated when firms improve their competitive positioning without any proactive (or, even, reactive) behaviour, but simply because of an environmental change driven by one, or some, of the other competitive forces present? This question, on the one hand, resonates with Alec Milne's challenging ideas (1961) about competition among animals, in which the focus on the environment (rather than on competition itself) is considered the core, in natural sciences, of the adaptation process.[2] The question, on the other, is also related to the concepts of dialectical thinking in general, and sense-making in particular, which we have illustrated in Chapter 1 (see pp. 8–9). In principle, one might argue that the firms' *inaction* prospected above can indeed be the consequence of a specific, precisely conscious form of enactment. In such a case, in other words, the top-decision makers of an enterprise could deliberately think that, to improve competitive positioning, inaction has to be preferred to action. At the same time, in Chapter 1, we have anticipated that, in principle, the ways in which enactment takes place, and its results, are guided by the co-evolutionary mix between the individuals' background, experience, and cognitive mechanisms (e.g., Cristofaro, 2022; Schiavone et al., 2024). However, what mix can specifically determine inaction still appears worth of investigation.

Third, when co-evolution is specifically considered, in Chapter 1 we have written that, at the beginning, this concept has been conceived, with the focus on firm level, as the joint, dynamic result of the interaction between strategic voluntarism and environmental determinism. Relatedly, we have written that, while, at the beginning, firms have mostly constituted the main unit of analysis, empirical inquiries on co-evolution have subsequently added other units at micro, meso, and macro levels (e.g., Abatecola et al., 2020). However, key questions regarding the understanding of co-evolutionary processes remain open. In particular, which is also somewhat related to the issues about enactment discussed above, *who* starts these processes? More specifically, and especially when firms are taken as the unit of analysis, how does the relationship between strategy and structure impact on co-evolution? Studying the relationship between firm's strategy and structure constitutes, as we know, one of the most investigated research areas in the field of strategic management. We also know that, over time, two juxtaposing perspectives have been substantially developed by scholars; on the one hand *structure follows strategy* and, on the other hand, *strategy follows structure*. In this regard, the pioneering work by Alfred Chandler (1962) on the evolution of many important firms in the US between 1919 and 1949 is globally acknowledged as the manifesto of the former perspective.[3] Conversely, since the 1970s studies proposing the latter perspective have also been developed. According to these studies (e.g., Bower, 1970; Hall and Saias, 1980), strategy follows structure because of the constraints that the latter enacts in the firm's decision-making process.

In the past century, indeed, some (somewhat more) co-evolutionary interpretations of the relationship have been also put forward. For example, according to Hrebiniak and Joyce (1984: 87): "Raising the directionality question amounts to the creation of a false dichotomy of causation and a resulting irrelevant dilemma [...] there is no satisfactory answer to this question because it is the question itself which is wrong". Likewise, according to Henry Mintzberg (1990: 187): "None take precedence, each always precedes the other and follows it [...] strategy formation is an integrated system, not an arbitrary sequence". We thus argue here that, also in line with the more general, subsequent development of co-evolutionary accounts explained in Chapter 1, new infusion to these interpretations could merit attention.

4.3 Enterprise early survival or mortality

In 1977, George Parks conjectures a model about enterprise evolution which can still result particularly useful to practitioners, in general, and entrepreneurs, in particular. In this model, the possible evolution of the life cycle of a firm conceptually draws on the traditional "S curve", which – as also recalled in the previous section – substantially means: (i) introduction; (ii) growth; (iii) maturity; (iv) decline. A key point of the model is that, in each of these phases, specific "hurdles" can take place, where hurdles can be considered as specific (and somewhat also not always anticipated) issues to be carefully monitored in a particular phase (Cafferata and Abatecola, 2017: 69–70). In principle, if happening, hurdles can strongly deviate the traditional revenues' curve of an enterprise below (or, conversely, also beyond in some cases) the level expected in a specific phase. The reason why Park's ideas have been chosen to open this section is that, especially as far as enterprise early survival (or mortality) is concerned, these ideas seemingly resonate with many arguments explained in Chapter 2 of this book. For example, in the introduction phase, a typical hurdle which Parks calls "start-up" can deal with – among others – the *lack of demand*,[4] thus with the difficulty to sell a good/service just introduced in the market because customers *de facto* do not appreciate it (see also Chapter 2, p. 23). Relatedly, in this phase, another common hurdle regards problems of "cash-flow", which often derive from the (still) low bargaining power of start-ups with suppliers on the one hand, and with customers on the other (see again Chapter 2, p. 25). In this regard, as Table 4.1 also shows, it is interesting to note that these hurdles are still among the most significant, recent determinants of start-ups' mortality.

The above introduced, a couple of other hurdles (i.e., "delegation" and "capitalization") occurring in the subsequent phase (growth) of the Parks's model merit, at least, attention. In particular, it is when we deal with these hurdles that we do not necessarily witness only a hurdle's negative effect on revenues. More specifically, the delegation hurdle regards the problems deriving from the separation between governance and management, with the associated delegation of authority necessary to support the growth phase. In terms of impact on performance, the (negative) impact of the delegation hurdle can still be considered similar to that of the hurdles previously illustrated. In fact, it is clear that, when the process of delegation is not positive as expected,

Table 4.1 Top reasons start-ups fail

Reason	*Percentage*
Ran out of cash/failed to raise new capital	38
No market need	35
Got outcompeted	20
Flawed business model	19
Regulatory/legal challenges	18
Pricing/cost issues	15
Not the right team	14
Product mistimed	10
Poor product	8
Disharmony among team/investors	7
Pivot gone bad	6
Burned out/lack of passion	5

Source: Adapted from CB Insights (2021).

Note: Based on analysis of 111 start-up *post-mortems* since 2018.

productivity and, as a consequence, also revenue problems almost always arise. Relatedly, the capitalization hurdle concerns problems in raising new capital to support the growth process (see again Table 4.1). *Sometimes*, however, the capitalization hurdle can also produce positive effects in terms of firm's growth. For example, as the historical evolution of many Unicorns mentioned in Table 4.2 suggests (see also Chapter 2, p. 26), this can happen when, during a particular round of investments, a start-up raises more capital than what it expects. It is clear that, if this happens, it is because investors particularly like the business idea (e.g., Wood and Wright, 2009; Lombardi et al., 2016), with the start-up's growth path then also increasing beyond the founding team's expectations.

All the considerations made so far in this section also resonate with other significant takeaways emerging from Chapter 2. More in general, also drawing on examples from the practice of entrepreneurship, Chapter 2 has offered a picture of how the research stream associated with Stinchcombe's "liability of newness" (1965) has evolved over time. In this regard, as explained, a difference can be individuated between what we could perceive as first (i.e., "smallness", "adolescence", "aging") and second (e.g., "foreignness", "ethnicity", "outsidership") *waves* of newness-related liability concepts gradually developed. In particular, while *first wave* liabilities mainly consider the effects of age per se on mortality rates, the focus of *second wave* liabilities regards more the effects of age on organizational learning, including behavioural and psychological determinants (e.g., Soto-Simeone et al., 2020). Chapter 2 has then ended with discussing Stinchcombe's construct of "imprinting"; in particular, this chapter has commented on how this construct has tremendously

Table 4.2 Top 10 Unicorn companies (May, 2024)

Company	*Valuation ($B)*	*Year joined*	*Country*	*Industry*	*Main investors*
Bytedance	225	2017	China	Media & Entertainment	Sequoia Capital China, SIG Asia Investments, Sina Weibo, SoftBank Group
SpaceX	200	2012	United States	Industrials	Founders Fund, Draper Fisher Jurvetson, Rothenberg Ventures
OpenAI	157	2019	United States	Enterprise Tech	Khosla Ventures, Thrive Capital, Sequoia Capital
Stripe	70	2014	United States	Financial Services	Khosla Ventures, LowercasecapitalG, capital
SHEIN	66	2018	Singapore	Consumer & Retail	Tiger Global Management, Sequoia Capital China, Shunwei Capital Partners
Revolut	45	2018	United Kingdom	Financial Services	Index Ventures, DST Global, Ribbit Capital
Databricks	43	2019	United States	Enterprise Tech	Andreessen Horowitz, New Enterprise Associates, Battery Ventures
Fanatics	31	2012	United States	Consumer & Retail	SoftBank Group, Andreessen Horowitz, Temasek Holdings
Canva	25.4	2018	Australia	Enterprise Tech	Sequoia Capital China, Blackbird Ventures, Matrix Partners
Epic Games	22.5	2018	United States	Media & Entertainment	Tencent Holdings, KKR, Smash Ventures

Source: Adapted from CB Insights (2024).

inspired the subsequent studies focusing on the influence of path dependence and self-reinforcing processes on the evolution of enterprises. As we put forward below, *combatting* the liability of newness on the one hand, and understanding imprinting on the other, can also merit some additional food for thought.

First, we know that, to date, the question is not whether Stinchcombe's "newness" (and newness-related, such as "smallness") assumptions still holds (e.g., Gimenez-Fernandez et al., 2020). In fact, the vast majority of firms continue to die young, with Unicorns and other kinds of high-growth start-ups being only exceptions (e.g., Giardino et al., 2023; Coad et al., 2024). Much more, the question still regards understanding what factors can help start-ups to survive the early selection period. In this regard, in Chapter 2, we have explained that the presence of certain elements, such as the experience and capabilities of the founder (one may think about *hero* entrepreneurs such as Arianna Huffington, Elon Musk, Oprah Winfrey, or Jeff Bezos) and of her/his founding team (e.g., Zahra et al., 2006; Shane, 2010), or the quality of the innovation (e.g., Ritala and Almpanopoulou, 2017; Scuotto et al., 2020) and entrepreneurial (e.g., Stam and Van de Ven, 2021) ecosystem, can surely help; however, more holistic, all variable-inclusive frameworks seem still needed.[5] For example, if we consider the impact of gender on entrepreneurial orientation and innovation propensity (e.g., Zannoni, 2024), past research has generally supported the idea that innovation is lower in women than in men-owned start-ups. However, a more exhaustive picture might emerge if also considering the kind of business and the degree of human capital and network ties available as well. As recently asserted, when all these factors are also observed, and especially when they appear similar, this picture appears more balanced (Mari et al., 2024).

Second (and related to the above), it also appears worthy of explanation here that entrepreneurial orientation is one thing, but disproportionate optimism is another thing; they have not to be confused. The latter, in fact, has been not rarely discovered to be a determinant of entrepreneurial early mortality (e.g., Hmieleski and Baron, 2009; Gudmundsson and Lechner, 2013) because of its capacity to decrease the rationality of judgement and decision-making. In this regard, when also looking at the behaviour of some entrepreneurs to date, one could thus ask whether, for example, certain kinds of personality and/or cultural dimensions can result in being specific antecedents of entrepreneurial optimism. In sum, considering personality/culture-related observations can seemingly constitute another support to the anticipated claim that more holistic explanatory frameworks are urged (e.g., Pereira et al., 2020; Pham et al., 2021), with these frameworks also embracing co-evolutionary perspectives (e.g., Baiocco et al., 2023). For example, as we have also explained in Chapter 2, according to Stinchcombe those start-ups which have successfully combatted their liability of newness often maintain their founding "imprint" (i.e., core DNA) during the subsequent phases of their life cycle. As argued by Stinchcombe, the main reason why this happens is that "traditionalizing forces, the vesting of interests, and the working out of ideologies may tend to preserve the structure" (1965: 169). One significant consequence of imprinting is, not rarely, resistance to radical change. On this side, we could thus question: (i) whether certain kinds of personality and/or cultural dimensions of the entrepreneur can foster (or reduce) imprinting; (ii) whether certain kinds of personality and/or cultural dimensions of the enterprise's human capital can serve as moderators; and (iii) what the co-evolutionary effect of the interaction between (i) and (ii) can be.

4.4 Enterprise failure and exit

Drawing on the study of a private British boarding school, in 1979 Andrew Pettigrew conceptualizes a model about enterprise evolution which, we believe, can also present many visible and invisible colleges with what we have explained, in Chapter 3 of this book, about enterprise failure and exit. In principle, one main pillar of the model is that, especially if observed with a long-term perspective, the life cycle of an enterprise can be conceived to be composed of the contemporaneous presence of: (i) long periods of routines and stability, and (ii) spotted periods (here and there) of governance and/or management "dramas" (Cafferata and Abatecola, 2017: 73–74). The concept of "drama" results key here; intended as a rare, isolated event of (mainly) social nature, a drama is potentially able to break routines and to foster radical strategic and/or organizational change. In this regard, the formal birth of an enterprise can be considered itself as a first example of drama. In fact, it is only when firms formally come to life that: (a) the routines associated with the pre-birth planning process end; (b) the selling of the firm's good or service really starts and, as a consequence, the entrepreneur can really have a feedback about the quality of her/his business idea. If the performance, especially in terms of financials, is much below what was expected, a radical change would then be urgently needed to avoid failure.[6] Subsequently, a second drama can happen when the historical founder of a company leaves and the succession takes place. The routines established during the founder's governance are, not rarely, put in question by the successor(s), as, especially in family business, many cases have often demonstrated.[7]

When discussing the Pettigrew's model with students, to explain dramas I (again) often use some facts from the Enron case. For example, as also previously illustrated in Chapter 3 (see pp. 45), a first drama (among others) at Enron can be said to date back to 1999, when the company launched its *private* stock exchange called "Enrononline". Enrononline very quickly led (and supports) the radical change of the company's core business, i.e., from the traditional production and distribution of energy to the much more sophisticated trading of financial derivatives related to energy commodities. Later on, a second drama can be said to take place in 2001. Written by journalist Bethany McLean in March, the *Fortune* article entitled "Is Enron Overpriced?" is the first to seriously raise concerns about what kind of economic and financial situation can really lie behind Enron's apparently outstanding performance. As we know, SEC (Securities and Exchange Commission) judicial inquiries quickly follow and, on December 2, 2001, Enron filed for Chapter 11 bankruptcy procedure; its stock value reached a peak of $90 per share in July and is now $0.26 per share worth.

The above explained, one may argue that Pettigrew's dramas also seemingly present much in common with the concept of "triggering event" illustrated in Chapter 3. In particular, when enterprises are concerned, we have explained the latter as an isolated event capable to transform the status of an already existing performance decline into that of a formal crisis. More specifically, as Chapter 3 has illustrated, the strategic management perspective considers corporate crises as the most evident phase of a cumulated process of competitiveness' decrease, often deriving from fallacies in the strategic planning and/or execution. When not timely arrested, this decrease translates into decline and, if amplified by an external or internal triggering event, finally into a crisis. Relatedly, Chapter 3 has explained that, in substance, decline and crisis never have only internal (i.e., firm-specific) or external (i.e., environmentally-driven) determinants; much more, they are almost always the result of the co-evolutionary relationship between the two (e.g., Schmitt et al., 2016); furthermore, the different weight of the two can be different according to the case. All these considerations can also merit additional food for thought, which we put forward below.

First, how can we measure the relevance of the crisis' determinants? Quantifying their importance, as written, not rarely appears challenging. In principle, for example, the analysis of those cases of corporate bankruptcy in which isolated, external factors appear as primary determinants seems easier than the study of those cases in which performance gradually, although constantly, deteriorates. No less important, the practice-based evidence has often suggested that theoretically differentiating decline and crisis, as two separate phases, is also per se not easy (e.g., Tangpong et al., 2015). In particular, this distinction appears problematic because one should be able to set a "non-returning point" (Guatri, 1995: 110), i.e., a threshold highlighting what level of economic and financial losses corresponds to decline, and what to crisis. We also argue here that individuating this threshold would be important not only to increase the quality of the *ex post* interpretative analyses but also of the *ex ante* default prediction modelling (e.g., Gordini, 2014; Gallucci et al., 2023).

Second, can specific socio-demographic and personality traits of the executives constitute an antecedent of corporate crises or, conversely, of successful corporate restructuring? More in general, can particular board features increase the survival chances of restructuring corporations? Some interesting answers to these questions have been already found over time. For example, as far as personality traits are concerned, it seems that turnaround firms led by emotionally stable Chief Executive Officers have higher survival chances than turnaround firms in which neurotic leaders take decisions (e.g., Abatecola et al., 2013). Relatedly, it seems that board independence can lead to positive effects (e.g., Dowell et al., 2011), while, as also anticipated in Chapter 3 (p. 49), the board replacement in general, and that of the Chief Executive Officer in particular, is not necessarily an appropriate solution per se.

Recently, attention has been also given to the empathy of Chief Executive Officers (Konig et al., 2020), from whose observation an inverted U-shaped pattern regarding their effectiveness in crisis management has emerged. However, it seems to us that, overall, these answers appear still fragmented to date;

thus, to understand the *big picture*, all-variable inclusive frameworks of observation might help also here. In this regard, we also claim that, because integrating psychology with strategic management theory and practice, behavioural strategy (Powell et al., 2011) can be an appropriate conceptual and methodological *dorsal spine* to build these frameworks. For example, behavioural strategy could help capture what psychological aspects can lead to the mentioned fallacy of strategic planning and/or execution, from which crises can ultimately derive. More specifically, it could help understand whether (and why) particular heuristics and/or decision-making traps can come to light and, then, can permanently remain in the cognitive mechanisms of the corporate top decision-makers (e.g., Cristofaro et al., 2024).

Third, we could also address the question of whether financial frauds need to be considered as a per se typology of crises. In other words, do the traditional crisis taxonomies and processes explained in Chapter 3 still hold? Or, instead, do we need a specific taxonomy when corporate executives are found to have consciously oriented their enterprises towards self-interest, rather than towards collective value for the shareholders and stakeholders? Since the Enron case at the beginning of this century, we have continued to witness financial frauds worldwide, with huge amounts of financial resources being stolen from innocent people (e.g., Rajan and Zingales, 2004; Greve et al., 2010). Corporate governance and accounting reforms have been – and are still being – implemented to combat them (e.g., Carretta and Mattarocci, 2013; Mechelli and Cimini, 2021). Yet, it seems that countervailing frauds still continues to occupy an important place in the institutional agenda of policymakers. We thus argue here that addressing this question could be important not only from a conceptual but also from a methodological point of view, because – we believe – it could perhaps help the increasing of frauds' detection and (hopefully) prevention (e.g., Han et al., 2024).

4.5 Avenues for practice

All that we have written in this book not only leads to the research avenues which we have outlined in the preceding sections of this chapter, but can also foster some (hopefully) useful "how to" implications for managers, entrepreneurs, and policymakers. We put them forward below.

4.5.1 Three keys to foster enterprise evolution

How can enterprises evolve and thrive? As explained so far, addressing this question has been a recurring theme of this book. Relatedly, addressing this question has been also central, for me, in many conversations within our evolutionary research group at the EURAM Annual Conference, with colleagues from the industry, and with students as well. In this regard, a possible, conceptual synthesis of what is illustrated in Chapter 1 – and whose implications have been further discussed in this chapter (pp. 66–69) – might flow as follows. Especially when conceived as *progress*, enterprise evolution should not be considered as driven solely by environmental (e.g., industrial) or strategic factors. Rather, it should be considered as a combination of the two. We know that, in the past, some strategic management or industrial organizations scholars were more extreme in advocating for one side or the other. At the same time, we believe three main practice-oriented takeaways can emerge here:

i *from evolution to co-evolution*: it can be important for managers to understand how the co-evolution between environmental forces and strategic proactivity impacts the firm's survival (e.g., Volberda and Lewin, 2003). Take our recent COVID-19 crisis disruptions. This was an unexpected shock. Firms seem more likely to survive over the long term if they adapt their capabilities to this shock. For example, well-known auto manufacturers can maintain profitability if they can flexibly convert their manufacturing in a way that counters the disruptions from COVID-19 (e.g. producing masks). The same can be true for all those restaurants able to convert their traditional value chain operations to provide pick-up and delivery services;

ii *board building*: I have to say that the term above has been gradually emerging, in my mind, also thanks to the classroom discussions with different audiences. From a leadership perspective, the term would mean that a key component for long-term survival is defining a corporate board with specific sociodemographic and personality variables (e.g., Ricciotti et al., 2022) or social skills (e.g., Sadun et al., 2022). As already explained widely in this book, this reflects the massive corpus of studies evolving around the "upper echelons" theory. For instance, there are numerous studies that demonstrate the benefits of having gender diversity on boards (e.g., Torchia et al., 2011). Or, we may consider that, from some aspects, company boards with a lower seniority rate seem more likely to survive a crisis;

iii *solve societal problems*: of course, I agree that the two above need to be combined to create solutions that still solve societal problems (e.g., Mazzucato, 2018; Paesano and Risso, 2024). While serving as a source of employment, goods or services that help humans with their basic needs also appear more likely to create "too big to fail" conditions, thus potentially benefitting from outside intervention if needed. For example, as anticipated in Chapter 3 (pp. 52), this seems what, among others, differentiated the US Government's reaction to the General Motors and Enron crises occurring at the end of the past century. The former received support because it was considered essential to the well-being of the country system; the second did not, because it was, to say it with Charles Darwin, (appropriately) considered *injurious*.

In sum, it seems that, especially in times of disruption, being proactive or inactive towards change is key in determining winners and losers in the competitive arena.

4.5.2 Three keys to unlock potential in start-ups

How can start-ups countervail the liability of newness? As explained so far, numerous statistics point to the stark reality that, at least in Europe and the US, the overwhelming majority of start-ups still die young. As explained in Chapter 2 – and whose implications have been further discussed in this chapter (pp. 69–72) – Stinchcombe's assumption (1965) is, in substance, still correct today: failure rates occur at the earliest stage of start-ups' life. At the same time, what can we learn from those outlier new ventures that survive and thrive? We believe that three main takeaways can emerge also here:

i *routines are required*: we have outlined that new companies often fail because they lack trust at different levels. At the internal level, this lack is often caused by the absence of established routines among the employees (e.g., Pentland et al., 2012; Breslin, 2022). This, of course, translates into (at least) temporary inefficiency, and ultimately low performance (e.g., Bendickson et al., 2017);

ii *adolescence matters*: we have explained that, about three decades ago, the "liability of adolescence" was also developed (see Chapter 2, pp. 27–30). In principle, this means that, after initial success called "honeymoon", a start-up can become complacent, with consequences that can be ultimately deadly. Conversely, trust, and associated early survival chances, can dramatically increase when the entrepreneur, or entrepreneurial team, adopts a long-term posture (e.g., Scafarto et al., 2019). In other words, s/he is able to accurately predict future market trends, and especially social needs, better than competitors;

iii *learn to fail*: we could have a particular perception of entrepreneurial success, on average: young individuals quitting school to launch innovative technology companies. The well-publicized stories of a young Mark Zuckerberg leaving Harvard to launch Facebook and Bill Gates dropping out of school to start Microsoft feed into this narrative. Indeed, these individuals are seemingly outliers; some research shows that the ideal age to launch a company is about 45 (e.g., Azoulay et al., 2018). By this time in life, the individual has often acquired more of the necessary skills and built the type of network that can serve as a foundation for long-term entrepreneurial success. Indeed, we believe, the capacity of learning (and growing) from (and through) previous failures is even more important than age. Again, in the words of Stinchcombe: "The main way to learn to form organizations is to form them. Beginning businessmen are more likely to succeed if they have failed before" (1965: 152).

Overall, it seems also clear that the items highlighted above can themselves nurture further ideas and dialogue. For example, we know that, especially if we consider the *human side of the coin* (e.g., Gambardella et al., 2015; Papa et al., 2020), routines can also be counterproductive because they can promote alienation and, ultimately, burnout. Relatedly, we know that entrepreneurial passion (e.g., Baraldi et al., 2020; Murphy, 2022) and intuition (e.g., Manesh et al., 2022) not only play a role in fostering long-term vision but can also co-evolve with entrepreneurial experience.

4.5.3 Three keys to survive a corporate crisis

How can corporate crises be prevented or combatted? As illustrated in Chapter 3 – and whose implications have been further discussed in this chapter (pp. 73–75), we could argue that there can be various ways in which an enterprise can consider the co-evolutionary dynamics that lead to crises, and thus develop the strategies to counter the environment:

i *forecasting is key:* companies need a focused group able to detect the warning signals happening in the environment, so they can deploy strategies to counter this. In large companies, this is often time a separate planning and forecasting department that constantly prepares data for the top management. Among the actions of this group should be in-depth, comprehensive scenario planning. This involves making assumptions on what the future business environment is going to be and how the organization, especially when conceived as a system, should respond to it (e.g., Golinelli, 2010; Barile, 2024). In terms of scenarios, it should consider the neutral (external variables remaining status quo), best-case (external variables evolving in a positive way), and worst-case (external variables evolving in a negative way). It is important to keep in mind that all three scenarios can occur. Based on data from these scenarios, the group should make predictions, keeping in mind that such prognostications can always be flawed (e.g., Felin et al., 2014);

ii *be wise*: another important approach to combatting crises with a co-evolutionary perspective seems to have a long-term view. The pressures to deliver quarterly earnings can lead to strategic decisions that do not consider the expectations of the external environment over the long term (e.g., Aguilera et al., 2007; Iandolo et al., 2024). Enron and WorldCom are just two of the many companies that have learned this lesson the hard way. Relatedly, we have mentioned many other examples of this in the United States, Europe, and even in Japan. On the contrary, a long-term perspective, in which the top management team responds to the data of different scenarios with its wisdom, can set up an organization to survive and potentially even thrive when a crisis emerges;

iii *board variables count*: finally, board characteristics can also reveal to be important to increase the survival chances of distressed firms. For example, research has found that board independence apparently matters (e.g., Abatecola et al., 2014) because it seemingly enhances objectivity, critical thinking, and rational problem solving. Conversely, and from some aspects (we might argue) also quite surprisingly, research has also shown that replacing the Chief Executive Officer during crisis situations, which is an action that most of the distressed companies do first, is a myth not necessarily per se positive to achieve successful corporate turnarounds. The empirical evidence shows that it works in some cases, while it does not in others. Other factors might determine whether this choice is appropriate or not.

To conclude, we have written that Enron's decision-making was impacted by greed, hubris, narcissism, and ego. A look around our chaotic world and we will perhaps perceive that many leaders in power did not seemingly get the memo about Enron's failures.

4.6 Summary

This chapter has outlined some implications for the research and practice regarding enterprise evolution, including early survival (or mortality), and failure and exit. Among those discussed, the main takeaways of the chapter could be summarized as follows.

First, with regard to the evolution of enterprises, we have written that understanding the relationship between exaptation and adaptation constitutes an interesting lively question (e.g., Santangelo and Stucchi, 2018; Aaltonen et al., 2020). With its parental domain also in natural sciences, exaptation, as explained, can be considered as that process for which, over time, the function of some organic features becomes different from the function for which these features were initially designed. Relatedly, we have explained that, when organizational adaptation is more generally observed (e.g., Cozzolino and Verona, 2024; Levinthal and Pham, 2024), another lively question regards understanding how it needs to be interpreted when firms ameliorate their competitive positioning substantially through *inaction*, i.e., without any reactive or proactive action in front of an environmental change. Further, when the relationship between firms and environments is again concerned (e.g., Jones and Walter, 2017), we have argued that addressing *who* – between the former and the latter – starts the co-evolutionary process merits further theoretical elaboration (e.g., Uli, 2018; Leoni and Cristofaro, 2022); in this regard, if we look inside firms, studying the relationship between strategy and structure would require symmetric observation.

Second, with regard to the early survival (or mortality) of enterprises, we have written that, to date, Stinchcombe's pioneering ideas (1965) about the liability of newness still substantially hold. Thus, the challenging question (much more) regards how to countervail newness and we claim that more holistic, co-evolutionary frameworks are urged here (e.g., Baiocco and Panic-cia, 2023). Relatedly, we have also claimed that co-evolution could be, both conceptually and methodologically, an appropriate basis to shed further light on Stinchcombe's notion of "imprinting", which substantially means the preservation, after the organizational early survival, of its core identity over the life cycle; as explained, imprinting has often given birth to organizational path dependence, with the latter also potentially happening at industry level (e.g., Belussi and Sedita, 2009; Marengo et al., 2023).

Third, with regard to the failure and exit of enterprises, we have argued that understanding whether certain socio-demographic and personality features of the top decision-makers can foster corporate crises (or turnarounds) would be probably of significant value. Specifically, as written, this understanding would be particularly important to capture potential causal relationships with the fallacy often regarding strategic planning/execution (e.g., Konig et al., 2020). Relatedly, and especially to enhance the possibilities of *ex ante* prevention, we have also claimed that understanding what threshold conceptually separates decline from crisis seems also important; in the former, strategic fallacy often appears still remediable, while, in the latter, it appears much more problematic from the beginning. This is also why, as thus observed, understanding whether financial frauds need to be considered as a specific form of crisis (e.g., Gundel, 2005), and whether they have to be managed differently from traditional ways, seems important; as the practice of business has sadly taught us, when frauds are discovered, the time passing between decline and failure is often very short.

In conclusion, this chapter can provide a contribution which is both conceptual and methodological. Conceptually, this chapter can help recognize how the various research items presented in the book can be theoretically considered as *pieces of the same puzzle*. Methodologically, this chapter can help recognize how these pieces can also form an important tool to understand how enterprises can thrive during different stages of their life cycle.

Notes

1 Progressively, the development of pen-drives and clouds also decreases this changed use, with the consequence of signing the substantial decline of the compact discs' industry as a whole.

2 "Competition is the endeavour of two (or more) animals to gain the same particular thing, or to gain the measure each wants from the supply of a thing when that supply is not sufficient for both (or all)" (Milne, 1961: 57).

3 "Structure follows strategy and the most complex type of structure is the result of the correlation of several basic strategies" (Chandler, 1962: 49).

4 "Do I really know enough about this type of business to be able to compete successfully with those who do?" (Parks, 1977: 27).
5 Furthermore, as we have also explained in Chapter 2, this need appears as even more evident especially if we move outside of US and/or Europe based observations.
6 This appears also why, from some aspects, this drama could be perceived as also owning some points in common with the first "hurdle" illustrated in the preceding section.
7 In family business, the succession moment is also not rarely associated with the occurring of what, more in general, has been called the "affect" heuristic (e.g., Cristofaro, 2019). This means that the founder does not *leave* to the member of the family who is really the most talented, but to the member of the family who s/he likes the most. Sometimes this member can also be the most talented, but sometimes not (e.g. Calabrò et al., 2018).

References

Aaltonen, P., Torkkeli, L. and Worek, M. (2020). 'The effect of emerging economies operations on knowledge utilization: The behavior of international companies as exaptation and adaptation'. In M. Marinov, S. Marinova, J. Larimo and T. Leposky (Eds.), *International business and emerging economy firms. Palgrave studies of internationalization in emerging markets.* Palgrave Macmillan, 49–87.

Abatecola, G., Breslin, D. and Kask, J. (2020). 'Do organizations really co-evolve? Problematizing co-evolutionary change in management and organization studies'. *Technological Forecasting and Social Change*, **155**, 119964.

Abatecola, G., Farina, V. and Gordini, N. (2014). 'Board effectiveness in corporate crises. Lessons from the evolving empirical research'. *Corporate Governance: The International Journal of Business in Society*, **14**(4), 531–542.

Abatecola, G., Mandarelli, G. and Poggesi, S. (2013). 'The personality factor: How top management teams make decisions. A literature review'. *Journal of Management and Governance*, **17**(4), 1073–1100.

Aguilera, R.V., Rupp, D.E., Williams, C.A. and Ganapathi, J. (2007). 'Putting the S back in corporate social responsibility: A multilevel theory of social change in organizations'. *Academy of Management Review*, **32**(3), 836–863.

Andriani, P. and Kaminska, R. (2021). 'Exploring the dynamics of novelty production through exaptation: A historical analysis of coal tar-based innovations'. *Research Policy*, **50**(2), 104171.

Ayres, R.U. and Steger, W.A. (1985). 'Rejuvenating the life cycle concept'. *Journal of Business Strategy*, **6**(1), 66–76.

Azoulay, P., Jones, B.F., Kim, J.D. and Miranda, J. (2018). 'The average age of a successful start-up founder is 45'. *Harvard Business Review*, July 11. Retrieved from https://hbr.org/2018/07/research-the-average-age-of-a-successful-startup-founder-is-45 (Last access: November 16, 2024).

Baiocco, S., Leoni, L. and Paniccia, P.M.A. (2023). 'Entrepreneurship for sustainable development: Co-evolutionary evidence from the tourism sector'. *Journal of Small Business and Enterprise Development*, **30**(7), 1521–1546.

Baiocco, S. and Paniccia, P.M.A. (2023). 'Business model innovation in sustainable entrepreneurship: Coevolutionary evidence from small accommodation firms'. *Business Process Management Journal*, **29**(8), 260–292.

Baraldi, E., Guercini, S., Lindahl, M. and Perna, A. (Eds., 2020). *Passion and entrepreneurship. Contemporary perspectives and new avenues for research*. Palgrave Macmillan.

Barile, S. (2024). *Systems thinking and viable systems*. Routledge.

Belussi, F. and Sedita, S.R. (2009). 'Life cycle vs. multiple path dependency in industrial districts'. *European Planning Studies*, **17**(4), 505–528.

Bendickson, J.S., Muldoon, J., Liguori, E.W. and Midgett, C. (2017). 'High performance work systems: A necessity for startups'. *Journal of Small Business Strategy*, 27(2), 1–12.

Bennett, R.C. and Cooper, R.G. (1984). 'The product life cycle trap'. *Business Horizons*, **27**(5), 7–16.

Bower, J.L. (1970). *Managing the resource allocation process: A study of corporate planning and investment.* Harvard Business School Press.

Breslin, D. (2022). 'When relationships get in the way: The emergence and persistence of care routines'. *Organization Studies*, **43**(12), 1869–1890.

Cafferata, R. and Abatecola, G. (2017). *Enterprise evolution. Teaching notes*. Texmat.

Calabrò, A., Minichilli, A., Amore, M.D. and Brogi, M. (2018). 'The courage to choose! Primogeniture and leadership succession in family firms'. *Strategic Management Journal*, **39**(7), 2014–2035.

Carretta, A. and Mattarocci, G. (Eds., 2013). *Financial systems in troubled waters. Information, strategies, and governance to enhance performance in risky times*. Routledge.

Cattani, G. and Mastrogiorgio, M. (Eds., 2021). *New developments in evolutionary innovation*. Oxford University Press.

CB Insights (2021). *The top 12 reasons start-ups fail*. Retrieved from https://www.cbinsights.com/research/report/startup-failure-reasons-top/ (Last access: November 4, 2024).

CB Insights (2024). *The complete list of Unicorn companies*. Retrieved from https://www.cbinsights.com/research-unicorn-companies (Last access: November 4, 2024).

Chandler, A.D. Jr. (1962). *Strategy and structure. Chapters in the history of the American industrial enterprise*. MIT Press.

Clarivate (2024). *'Sleeping beauties': Yesterday's findings fuel today's research breakthroughs*. Report.

Coad, A., Bornhäll, A., Daunfeldt, S.-O. and McKelvie, A. (2024). *Scale-ups and high-growth firms. Theory, definitions, and measurement.* Springer.

Cozzolino, A. and Verona, G. (2024). 'Decision tree for adaptation after radical changes: Linking dynamic capabilities, ambidexterity, and strategic alliances'. *Journal of Management and Governance*, **28**, 745–769.

Cristofaro, M. (2019). 'The role of affect in management decision: A systematic review'. *European Management Journal*, **37**(1), 6–17.

Cristofaro, M. (2022). 'Organizational sensemaking: A systematic review and a coevolutionary model'. *European Management Journal*, **40**(3), 393–405.

Cristofaro, M., Augier, M., Lovallo, D., Abatecola, G. and Leoni, L. (2024). 'Behavioral strategy in evolution: A review and conceptual framework'. *European Management Journal*, https://doi.org/10.1016/j.emj.2024.10.002.

Dew, N. and Sarasvathy, S.D. (2016). 'Exaptation and niche construction: Behavioral insights for an evolutionary theory'. *Industrial and Corporate Change*, **25**(1), 167–179.

Dowell, G.W.S., Shackell, M.B. and Stuart, N.V. (2011). 'Boards, CEOs, and surviving a crisis: Evidence from the Internet shakeout'. *Strategic Management Journal*, **32**(10), 1025–1045.

Felin, T., Kauffman, S., Koppl, R. and Longo, G. (2014). 'Economic opportunity and evolution: Beyond landscapes and bounded rationality'. *Strategic Entrepreneurship Journal*, **8**(4), 269–282.

Gallucci, C., Santulli, R., Modina, M. and Formisano, V. (2023). 'Financial ratios, corporate governance and bank-firm information: A Bayesian approach to predict SMEs' default'. *Journal of Management and Governance*, **27**(3), 873–892.

Gambardella, A., Panico, C. and Valentini, G. (2015). 'Strategic incentives to human capital'. *Strategic Management Journal*, **36**(1), 37–52.

Garud, R., Gehman, J. and Giuliani, A.P. (2016). 'Technological exaptation: A narrative approach'. *Industrial and Corporate Change*, **25**(1), 149–166.

Giardino, P., Delladio, S., Baiocco, S. and Caputo, A. (2023). 'Beyond myth: A systematic literature review on the emergence of unicorn firms'. *Journal of Small Business and Enterprise Development*, **30**(6), 1156–1177.

Gimenez-Fernandez, E.M., Sandulli, F.D. and Bogers, M. (2020). 'Unpacking liabilities of newness and smallness in innovative start-ups: Investigating the differences in innovation performance between new and older small firms'. *Research Policy*, **49**(10), 104049.

Golinelli, G.M. (2010). *Viable Systems Approach (VSA). Governing business dynamics*. CEDAM.

Gordini, N. (2014). 'A genetic algorithm approach for SME bankruptcy prediction: Empirical evidence from Italy'. *Expert Systems with Applications*, **41**(14), 6433–6445.

Gould, S.J. and Vrba, E.S. (1982). 'Exaptation. A missing term in the science of form'. *Paleobiology*, **8**(3), 4–15.

Greve, H.R., Palmer, D. and Pozner, J.-E. (2010). 'Organizations gone wild: The causes, processes, and consequences of organizational misconduct'. *Academy of Management Annals*, **4**(1), 53–107.

Guatri, L. (1995). *Turnaround. Declino, crisi e ritorno al valore*. EGEA.

Gudmundsson, S.V. and Lechner, C. (2013). 'Cognitive biases, organization, and entrepreneurial firm survival'. *European Management Journal*, **31**(3), 278–294.

Gundel, S. (2005). 'Towards a new typology of crises'. *Journal of Contingencies and Crisis Management*, **13**(3), 106–115.

Hall, D.J. and Saias, M.A. (1980). 'Strategy follows structure!'. *Strategic Management Journal*, **1**(2), 149–163.

Han, J.-H., Pollock, T.G and Graffin, S.D. (2024). 'Now you see me: How status and categorical proximity shape misconduct scandalization'. *Academy of Management Journal*, **67**(1), 208–231.

Hmieleski, K.M. and Baron, R.A. (2009). 'Entrepreneurs' optimism and new venture performance: A social cognitive perspective'. *Academy of Management Journal*, **52**(3), 473–488.

Hrebiniak, L.G. and Joyce, W.F. (1984). *Implementing strategy*. Macmillan.

Iandolo, F., La Sala, A., Turriziani, L. and Caputo, F. (2024). 'Stakeholder engagement in managing systemic risk management'. *Business Ethics, the Environment & Responsibility*, https://doi.org/10.1111/beer.12694.

Jones, C. and Walter, G. (2017). *An autecological theory of the firm and its environment*. Edward Elgar.

Konig, A.S., Graf-Vlachy, L., Bundy, J.N. and Little, L. (2020). 'A blessing and a curse: How CEOs' empathy affects their management of organizational crises'. *Academy of Management Review*, **45**(1), 130–153.

Leoni, L. and Cristofaro, M. (2022), 'To adopt or not to adopt? A co-evolutionary framework and paradox of technology adoption by small museums'. *Current Issues in Tourism*, **25**(18), 2969–2990.

Levinthal, D.A. and Pham, D.N. (2024). 'Bringing politics back in: The role of power and coalitions in organizational adaptation'. *Organization Science*, **35**(5), 1704–1720.

Levitt, T. (1965). 'Exploit the product life cycle'. *Harvard Business Review*, **43**(6), 81–94.

Lombardi, R., Trequattrini, R. and Russo, G. (2016). 'Innovative start-ups and equity crowd-funding'. *International Journal of Risk Assessment and Management*, **19**(1–2), 68–83.

Manesh, M.F., Flamini, G., Petrolo, D. and Palumbo, R. (2022). 'A round of dancing and then one more: Embedding intuition in the ballet of entrepreneurial decision making'. *International Entrepreneurship and Management Journal*, **18**(2), 499–528.

Marengo, L., Settepanella, S. and Valente, M. (2023). 'Mendelian explorations'. *Journal of Organization Design*, **12**, 157–163.

Mari, M., Poggesi, S., Abatecola, G. and Essers, C. (2024). 'Women entrepreneurs and innovation: Retrospect and prospect'. *Journal of Innovation & Knowledge*, **9**(3), 100519.

Mazzucato, M. (2018). *The value of everything. Making and taking in the global economy*. Penguin Books.

McLean, B. (2001). 'Is Enron Overpriced?'. *Fortune*, March 5.

Mechelli, A. and Cimini, R. (2021). 'The effect of corporate governance and investor protection environments on the value relevance of new accounting standards: The case of IFRS 9 and IAS 39'. *Journal of Management and Governance*, **25**(4), 1241–1266.

Milne, A. (1961). 'Definition of competition among animals'. In F.L. Milnethorpe (Ed.), *Mechanisms in biological competition*. Cambridge University Press, 40–61.

Mintzberg, H. (1990). 'The Design School: Reconsidering the basic premises of strategic management'. *Strategic Management Journal*, **11**(3), 171–195.

Murphy, P.J. (2022). 'Editorial: Passion: An entrepreneurial constant'. *Journal of Small Business and Enterprise Development*, **29**(7), 993–993.

Paesano, A. and Risso, M. (2024). 'A synergy of spirituality and technologies toward a society 5.0'. In M. Del Baldo, M.G. Baldarelli and E. Righini (Eds.), *Place based approaches to sustainability volume II. Business, economics, and social models*. Palgrave Macmillan, 143–175.

Paniccia, P.M.A. and Leoni, L. (2019). 'Co-evolution in tourism: The case of albergo diffuso'. *Current Issues in Tourism*, **22**(10), 1216–1243.

Papa, A., Dezi, L., Gregori, G.L., Mueller, J. and Miglietta, N. (2020). 'Improving innovation performance through knowledge acquisition: The moderating role of employee retention and human resource management practices'. *Journal of Knowledge Management*, **24**(3), 589–605.

Parks, G.M. (1977). 'How to climb a growth curve: Eleven hurdles for the entrepreneur-manager'. *Journal of Small Business Management*, **15**(1), 25–29, and **15**(2), 45–49.

Pentland, B.T., Feldman, M.S., Becker, M.C. and Liu, P. (2012). 'Dynamics of organizational routines: A generative model'. *Journal of Management Studies*, **49**(8), 1484–1508.

Pereira, V., Corradini, C., Temouri, Y. and Mellahi, K. (2020). 'Investigating institutional, economic and social determinants of European regions for firm growth through employment generation'. *British Journal of Management*, **31**(1), 162–183.

Pettigrew, A.M. (1979). 'On studying organizational cultures'. *Administrative Science Quarterly*, **24**(4), 570–581.

Pham, D., Jones, P., Dobson, S., Linan, F. and Viala, C. (2021). 'Entrepreneurial implementation intention as a tool to moderate the stability of entrepreneurial goal intention: A sensemaking approach'. *Journal of Business Research*, **123**, 97–105.

Powell, T.C., Lovallo, D. and Fox, C.R. (2011). 'Behavioral strategy'. *Strategic Management Journal*, **32**(13), 1369–1386.

Rajan, R.G. and Zingales, L. (2004). *Saving capitalism from the capitalists. Unleashing the power of financial markets to create wealth and spread opportunity*. Princeton University Press.

Ricciotti, F., Cristofaro, M., Abatecola, G. and Mari, M. (2022). 'Executive profiles and performance of real estate services: Evidence of *reverse causality* from Europe'. *Cities*, **130**, 103854.

Ritala, P. and Almpanopoulou, A. (2017). 'In defense of "eco" in innovation ecosystem'. *Techovation*, **60–61**, 39–42.

Sadun, R., Fuller, J.B., Hansen, S. and Neal, P.J. (2022). 'The C-Suite skills that matter most'. *Harvard Business Review*, **100**(4), 42–50.

Santangelo, G.D. and Stucchi, T. (2018). 'Internationalization through exaptation: The role of domestic geographical dispersion in the internationalization process'. *Journal of International Business Studies*, **49**(6), 753–760.

Scafarto, F., Poggesi, S. and Mari, M. (2019). 'Entrepreneurial intentions, risk-taking propensity and environmental support: The Italian experience'. In A. Caputo and M.M. Pellegrini (Eds.), *The anatomy of entrepreneurial decisions. Past, present and future research directions*. Springer, 218–231.

Schiavone, F., Zeuli, F., Perillo, C. and Bastone, A. (2024). 'Enhancing sense-making through intellectual capital: Evidence from a healthcare network'. *Journal of Innovation & Knowledge*, **9**(4), 100619.

Schmitt, A., Barker, V.L., Raisch, S. and Whetten, D. (2016). 'Strategic renewal in times of environmental scarcity'. *Long Range Planning*, **49**(3), 361–376.

Scuotto, V., Garcia-Perez, A., Cillo, V. and Giacosa, E. (2020). 'Do stakeholder capabilities promote sustainable business innovation in small and medium-sized enterprises? Evidence from Italy'. *Journal of Business Research*, **119**, 131–141.

Shane, S. (2010). *Born entrepreneurs, born leaders. How your genes affect your work life*. Oxford University Press.

Simone, C., Barile, S. and Grandinetti, R. (2021). 'The emergence of new market spaces: Brokerage and firm cognitive endowment'. *Journal of Business Research*, **134**(4), 457–466.

Soto-Simeone, A., Sirén, C. and Antretter, T. (2020). 'New venture survival: A review and extension'. *International Journal of Management Reviews*, **22**(4), 378–407.

Stam, E. and Van de Ven, A.H. (2021). 'Entrepreneurial ecosystem elements'. *Small Business Economics*, **56**, 809–832.

Stinchcombe, A.L. (1965). 'Social structure and organizations'. In J. March (Ed.), *Handbook of organizations*. Rand McNally, 142–193.

Tangpong, C., Abebe, M. and Li, Z. (2015). 'A temporal approach to retrenchment and successful turnaround in declining firms'. *Journal of Management Studies*, **52**(5), 647–677.

Torchia, M., Calabrò, A. and Huse, M. (2011). 'Women directors on corporate boards: From Tokenism to critical mass'. *Journal of Business Ethics*, 102, 299–317.

Uli, V. (2018). 'A multilevel co-evolutionary perspective on organizational adaptation. Evidence from the service industry'. *Business Process Management Journal*, **24**(3), 652–670.

Volberda, H.K. and Lewin, A. (2003). 'Co-evolutionary dynamics within and between firms: From evolution to co-evolution'. *Journal of Management Studies*, **40**(8), 2111–2136.

Volpato, G. (2009). 'Fiat Group Automobiles - An Arabian phoenix in the international auto industry'. In M. Freyssenet (Ed.), *The second automobile revolution – Trajectories of the world carmakers in the 21st century*. Palgrave Macmillan, 287–308.

Wood, G. and Wright, M. (2009). 'Private equity: A review and synthesis'. *International Journal of Management Reviews*, **11**(4), 361–380.

Zahra, S.A, Sapienza, H.J. and Davidsson, P. (2006). 'Entrepreneurship and dynamic capabilities: A review, model and research agenda'. *Journal of Management Studies*, **43**(4), 917–955.

Zannoni, A. (2024). 'Reviewing the gender gap in management and entrepreneurship: Environmental factors and co-evolutionary dynamics'. *International Journal of Globalisation and Small Business*, **14**(2), 138–167.

Conclusion

Everyday business co-evolves with competition. In a split second, firms can come to light or are *selected out*. Disruption is impacting every industry and type of enterprise. Age, dimension, cultural context, or ownership no longer seem to guarantee survival per se. But it is not all gloom and doom. Healthy firms do matter for the well-being of society and, among others, this review book has attempted to provide a contribution about the keys to surviving and evolving in our turbulent times. Although mostly research-based, the narrative style used, together with the real-world examples from the practice of business, have been thought to connect colleagues both from academia and industry, policymakers, and students.

Especially if we consider a practice-oriented perspective, in relation to which the term "Businesstype" has been also introduced in the last book chapter, the book has substantially revolved around three main, intertwined questions: *How can enterprises evolve? How can start-ups survive? How can enterprises combat crises?* As far as enterprise evolution is concerned, the book has explained that, from more than one aspect, we can compare competition in biology and firm survival over time. In this regard, this book has highlighted the importance of *building boards* that prioritize the satisfaction of social needs; to this purpose, the boards' capacity to adopt strategic perspectives which appear less self-referential and more *co-evolutionary* would be key. In parallel, as far as enterprise early survival (or mortality) is concerned, the book has stressed that death rates among start-ups are (still) very high; yet, outliers exist. To this end, the book has highlighted the importance, among others, of establishing appropriate and well-balanced (from a human point of view) operational routines to save time (and, thus, gaining efficiency); this, of course, cannot avoid going in parallel with adopting a long-term entrepreneurial vision based on the *learning to fail* attitude. Finally, as for enterprise failure and exit, the book has claimed that, when suffering a corporate crisis, right choices can lead to new prosperity. To this scope, the book has highlighted the importance of adopting suitable forecasting techniques, together with (evergreen) strategic wisdom; *board building* seemingly counts also here, with

DOI: 10.4324/9781003412663-5

heterogeneity and independence resulting as a potential tool to contrast substantive fallacies and biases in executive decision-making.

In conclusion, while conjecturing this review book, one main goal was to provide readers from strategic management (and, from more than one aspect, entrepreneurship as well) with a perhaps more integrated picture about key themes regarding enterprise evolution, which are often observed through a more single-focused lens. It is clear that the book does not intend to be exhaustive and that, quoting Andrew Pettigrew (1979: 580), it has still "only listed some items on a menu and put some of the items together in some simple dishes; it remains for others to broaden the menu and produce the cordon bleu meals".

In parallel, and as another final, personal consideration, this book sees light when I am in my mid-forties; however, as explained in its Preface, I started to plan (and write) its contents many years ago. Reflecting on this not only resonates with Charles Darwin's unforgotten legacy that evolution is slow, gradual, and constant, but also resonates with my undoubtful feeling that, while writing, the book's final contents have gradually co-evolved with my life as a person, husband, father, and professor of management.

Reference

Pettigrew, A.M. (1979). 'On studying organizational cultures'. *Administrative Science Quarterly*, **24**(4), 570–581.

Bibliography

Aaltonen, P., Torkkeli, L. and Worek, M. (2020). 'The effect of emerging economies operations on knowledge utilization: The behavior of international companies as exaptation and adaptation'. In M. Marinov, S. Marinova, J. Larimo and T. Leposky (Eds.), *International business and emerging economy firms. Palgrave studies of internationalization in emerging markets*. Palgrave Macmillan, 49–87.

Abatecola, G. (2007). *Crisi d'impresa. Elementi di teoria e evidenze empiriche*. Aracne.

Abatecola, G. (2012). 'Organizational adaptation. An update'. *International Journal of Organizational Analysis*, **20**(3), 274–293.

Abatecola, G. (2012). 'Interpreting corporate crises: Towards a co-evolutionary approach'. *Futures*, **44**(10), 860–869.

Abatecola, G. (2014). 'Research in organizational evolution. What comes next?' *European Management Journal*, **32**(3), 434–443.

Abatecola, G. (2014). 'Untangling self-reinforcing processes in managerial decision making. Co-evolving heuristics?'. *Management Decision*, **52**(2), 934–949.

Abatecola, G. (2019). 'Reviewing corporate crises: A strategic management perspective'. *International Journal of Business and Management*, **14**(5): 21–31.

Abatecola, G., Breslin, D. and Kask, J. (2020). 'Do organizations really co-evolve? Problematizing co-evolutionary change in management and organization studies'. *Technological Forecasting and Social Change*, **155**, 119964.

Abatecola, G., Cafferata, R. and Poggesi, S. (2012). 'Arthur Stinchcombe's *Liability of Newness*. Contribution and Impact of the Construct'. *Journal of Management History*, **18**(4), 402–418.

Abatecola, G., Farina, V. and Gordini, N. (2014). 'Board effectiveness in corporate crises. Lessons from the evolving empirical research'. *Corporate Governance: The International Journal of Business in Society*, **14**(4), 531–542.

Abatecola, G., Mandarelli, G., Poggesi, S. (2013). 'The personality factor: How top management teams make decisions. A literature review'. *Journal of Management and Governance*, **17**(4), 1073–1100.

Abatecola, G., Mari, M. and Poggesi, S. (2020). 'How can virtuous real estate public-private partnerships be developed? Towards a co-evolutionary perspective'. *Cities*, **107**, 102896.

Acciarini, C., Brunetta, F. and Boccardelli, P. (2021). 'Cognitive biases and decision-making strategies in times of change: A systematic literature review'. *Management Decision*, **59**(3), 638–652.

Adinolfi, P. (2021). 'A journey around decision-making: Searching for the "big picture" across disciplines'. *European Management Journal*, **39**(1), 9–21.

Adriaanse, J. (2017). 'Back to the future: The General Motors restructuring plan'. In J. Adriaanse and J.P. van der Rest (Eds.), *Turnaround management and bankruptcy*. Routledge, 365–387.

Adriaanse, J. and van der Rest, J.P. (Eds., 2017). *Turnaround management and bankruptcy*. Routledge.

Aguilera, R.V., Rupp, D.E., Williams, C.A. and Ganapathi, J. (2007). 'Putting the S back in corporate social responsibility: A multilevel theory of social change in organizations'. *Academy of Management Review*, **32**(3), 836–863.

Aldrich, H.E. and Auster, E.R. (1986). 'Even dwarfs started small: Liabilities of age and size and their strategic implications'. *Research in Organizational Behaviour*, **8**(2), 165–198.

Aldrich, H.E. and Ruef, M. (2018). 'Unicorns, gazelles, and other distractions on the way to understanding real entrepreneurship in the United States'. *Academy of Management Perspectives*, **32**(4), 458–472.

Aldrich, H.E., Ruef, M. and Lippmann, S. (2020). *Organizations evolving* (3rd edition). Edward Elgar.

Almudi, I. and Fatas-Villafranca, F. (2021). *Co-evolution in economic systems*. Cambridge University Press.

Altman, R. (1968). 'Financial ratios. Discriminant analysis and the prediction of corporate bankruptcy'. *Journal of Finance*, **23**(4), 589–609.

Andriani, P. and Kaminska, R. (2021). 'Exploring the dynamics of novelty production through exaptation: A historical analysis of coal tar-based innovations'. *Research Policy*, **50**(2), 104171.

Argenti, J. (1976). *Corporate collapse. The cause and symptoms*. McGraw-Hill.

Arthur, W.B. (1994). *Increasing returns and path dependence in the economy*. University of Michigan Press.

Astley, W.G. and Van de Ven, A.H. (1983). 'Central perspectives and debates in organization theory'. *Administrative Science Quarterly*, **28**(2), 245–273.

Audretsch, D.B., Aronica, M., Belitski, M. and Piacentino, D. (2024). 'Natural selection or strategic adaptation? Entrepreneurial digital technologies and survival of the species'. *Journal of Technology Transfer*, **49**, 1631–1659.

Ayres, R.U. and Steger, W.A. (1985). "Rejuvenating the life cycle concept'. *Journal of Business Strategy*, **6**(1), 66–76.

Azoulay, P., Jones, B.F., Kim, J.D. and Miranda, J. (2018). 'The average age of a successful start-up founder is 45'. *Harvard Business Review*, July 11. Retrieved from https://hbr.org/2018/07/research-the-average-age-of-a-successful-startup-founder-is-45 (Last access: November 16, 2024).

Baiocco, S., Leoni, L. and Paniccia, P.M.A. (2023). 'Entrepreneurship for sustainable development: Co-evolutionary evidence from the tourism sector'. *Journal of Small Business and Enterprise Development*, **30**(7), 1521–1546.

Baiocco, S. and Paniccia, P.M.A. (2023). 'Business model innovation in sustainable entrepreneurship: Coevolutionary evidence from small accommodation firms'. *Business Process Management Journal*, **29**(8), 260–292.

Baraldi, E., Guercini, S., Lindahl, M. and Perna, A. (Eds., 2020). *Passion and entrepreneurship. Contemporary perspectives and new avenues for research*. Palgrave Macmillan.

Barbero, J.L., Di Pietro, F. and Chiang, C. (2017). 'A rush of blood to the head: Temporal dimensions of retrenchment, environment and turnaround performance'. *Long Range Planning*, **50**(6), 862–879.

Barile, S. (2024). *Systems thinking and viable systems*. Routledge.

Barmash, I. (Ed., 1973). *Great business disasters. Swindlers, bunglers and frauds in American industry*. Ballantine Books.

Barron, D.N., West, E. and Hannan, M.T. (1994). 'A time to grow and a time to die: Growth and mortality of credit unions in New York city: 1914-1990'. *American Journal of Sociology*, **100**(2), 381–421.

Baum, J.A.C. (1996). 'Organizational ecology'. In S.R. Clegg, C. Hardy and W. Nord (Eds.), *Handbook of organization studies*. Sage, 77–114.

Baum, J.A.C. and Singh, J.V. (1994). 'Organization-environment co-evolution'. In J.A.C. Baum and J.V. Singh (Eds.), *Evolutionary dynamics of organizations*. Oxford University Press, 379–402.

Becker, M.C. (2004). 'Organizational routines: A review of the literature'. *Industrial and Corporate Change*, **13**(4), 643–677.

Bedeian, A.G. (2006). 'Choice and determinism. A comment'. *Strategic Management Journal*, **11**(7), 571–573.

Bellavitis, C., Rietveld, J. and Filatotchev, I. (2020). 'The effects of prior co-investments on the performance of venture capitalist syndicates: A relational agency perspective'. *Strategic Entrepreneurship Journal*, **14**(2), 240–264.

Belussi, F. and Sedita, S.R. (2009). 'Life cycle vs. multiple path dependency in industrial districts'. *European Planning Studies*, **17**(4), 505–528.

Bendickson, J.S., Muldoon, J., Liguori, E.W. and Midgett, C. (2017). 'High performance work systems: A necessity for startups'. *Journal of Small Business Strategy*, 27(2), 1–12.

Benevolo, C., Penco, L. and Torre, T. (2021). 'Entrepreneurial decision-making for global strategies: A "heart–head" approach'. *Management Decision*, **59**(5), 1132–1157.

Bennett, R.C. and Cooper, R.G. (1984). 'The product life cycle trap'. *Business Horizons*, **27**(5), 7–16.

Benson, J.K. (1977). 'Organizations: A dialectical view'. *Administrative Science Quarterly*, **22**(1), 1–21.

Bibeault, D.B. (1982). *Corporate turnaround. How managers turn losers into winners*. McGraw-Hill.

Bibeault, D. (2017). 'The history of corporate turnaround. Personal reflections'. In J. Adriaanse and J.P. van der Rest (Eds.), *Turnaround management and bankruptcy*. Routledge, 3–21.

Billings, R.S., Milburn, T.W. and Schaalman, M.L. (1980). 'A model of crisis perception: A theoretical and empirical analysis'. *Administrative Science Quarterly*, **25**(8), 300–316.

Bourgeois, L.J. III (1984). 'Strategic management and determinism'. *Academy of Management Review*, **9**(4), 586–596.

Bowden, B. (2017). 'An exploration into the relationship between management and market forces: The railroads of Australia and the American West, 1880-1900'. *Journal of Management History*, **23**(3), 297–314.

Bower, J.L. (1970). *Managing the resource allocation process: A study of corporate planning and investment.* Harvard Business School Press.

Breslin, D. (2011). 'Reviewing a generalized Darwinist approach to studying socio-economic change'. *International Journal of Management Reviews*, **13**(2), 218–235.

Breslin, D. (2022). 'When relationships get in the way: The emergence and persistence of care routines'. *Organization Studies*, **43**(12), 1869–1890.

Breslin, D., Kask, J., Schlaile, M. and Abatecola, G. (2021). 'Developing a co-evolutionary account of innovation ecosystems'. *Industrial Marketing Management*, **98**, 59–68.

Brown, A.D. and Starkey, K. (2000). 'Organizational identity and organizational learning: A psychodynamic perspective'. *Academy of Management Review*, **25**(1), 102–120.

Brüderl, J. and Schüssler, R. (1990). 'Organizational mortality: The liabilities of newness and adolescence'. *Administrative Science Quarterly*, **35**(3), 530–547.

Brunelli, S. and Di Carlo, E. (Eds., 2020). *Accountability, ethics and sustainability of organizations. New theories, strategies and tools for survival and growth*. Springer.

Brusoni, S. and Prencipe, A. (2006). 'Making design rules: A multidomain perspective'. *Organization Science*, **17**(2), 179–189.

Bundy, J., Pfarrer, M.D., Short, C.E. and Coombs, W.T. (2017). 'Crises and crisis management: Integration, interpretation, and research development'. *Journal of Management*, **43**(6), 1661–1692.

Burgelman, R.A. (1991). 'Intra-organizational ecology of strategy making and organizational adaptation: Theory and field research'. *Organization Science*, **2**(3), 239–262.

Burgelman, R.A., Snihur, Y. and Thomas, L.D.W. (2023). *Strategy-making and organizational evolution. A managerial agency perspective*. Cambridge University Press.

Cafferata, R. (2016). 'Darwinist connections between the systemness of social organizations and their evolution'. *Journal of Management and Governance*, **20**(1), 19–44.

Cafferata, R. (2022). *Management in adattamento. Tra razionalità economica, evoluzione ed imperfezione dei sistemi* (3rd edition). Il Mulino.

Cafferata, R. and Abatecola, G. (2017). *Enterprise evolution. Teaching notes*. Texmat.

Calabrò, A., Minichilli, A., Amore, M.D. and Brogi, M. (2018). 'The courage to choose! Primogeniture and leadership succession in family firms'. *Strategic Management Journal*, **39**(7), 2014–2035.

Cameron K.A., Sutton R.I. and Whetten, A.D. (Eds., 1988). *Readings in organizational* dec*line: Frameworks, research and prescriptions*. Ballinger.

Campbell, D. (1965). 'Variation, selection and retention in sociocultural evolution'. In H.R. Barringer, G.I. Blanksten and R.W. Mack (Eds.), *Social change in developing areas: A reinterpretation of evolutionary theory*. Schenkman, 19–49.

Campopiano, G., De Massis, A., Rinaldi, F.R. and Sciascia, S. (2017). 'Women's involvement in family firms: Progress and challenges for future research'. *Journal of Family Business Strategy*, **8**(4), 200–212.

Capaldo, P. (1977). 'Crisi d'impresa e suo risanamento'. *Banche e Banchieri*, **5**, 315–329.

Caputo, A. and Pellegrini, M.M. (Eds., 2019). *The anatomy of entrepreneurial decisions: Past, present and future research directions*. Springer Nature.

Carney, M. and Dieleman, M. (2024). 'See who I know! Addressing the liabilities of outsidership through status signaling'. *Journal of International Business Studies*, **55**, 377–395.

Carretta, A. and Mattarocci, G. (Eds., 2013). *Financial systems in troubled waters. Information, strategies, and governance to enhance performance in risky times*. Routledge.

Carroll, G.R. (1983). 'A stochastic model of organizational mortality: Review and reanalysis'. *Social Science Research*, **12**(4), 303–329.

Cattani, G. and Mastrogiorgio, M. (Eds., 2021). *New developments in evolutionary innovation*. Oxford University Press.

CB Insights (2021). *The top 12 reasons start-ups fail.* Retrieved from https://www.cbinsights.com/research/report/startup-failure-reasons-top/ (Last access: November 4, 2024).

CB Insights (2024). *The complete list of Unicorn companies.* Retrieved from https://www.cbinsights.com/research-unicorn-companies (Last access: November 4, 2024).

Cepiku, D., Giordano, F., Mastrodascio, M. and Wang, W. (2021). 'What drives network effectiveness? A configurational approach'. *Public Management Review*, **23**(10), 1479–1503.

Chandler, A.D. Jr. (1962). *Strategy and structure. Chapters in the history of the American industrial enterprise*. MIT Press.

Child, J. (1972). 'Organizational structure, environment and performance: The role of strategic choice'. *Sociology*, **6**(1), 1–22.

Child, J. (1997). 'Strategic choice in the analysis of action, structure, organization and the environment: Retrospect and prospect'. *Organization Studies*, **18**(1), 43–76.

Clarivate (2024). *'Sleeping beauties': Yesterday's findings fuel today's research breakthroughs*. Report.

Coad, A., Bornhäll, A., Daunfeldt, S.-O. and McKelvie, A. (2024). *Scale-ups and high-growth firms. Theory, definitions, and measurement*. Springer.

Coad, A. and Storey, D. (2021). 'Taking the entrepreneur out of entrepreneurship'. *International Journal of Management Reviews*, **23**(4), 541–548.

Cozzolino, A. and Verona, G. (2024). 'Decision tree for adaptation after radical changes: Linking dynamic capabilities, ambidexterity, and strategic alliances'. *Journal of Management and Governance*, **28**, 745–769.

Cristofaro, M. (2019). 'The role of affect in management decision: A systematic review'. *European Management Journal*, **37**(1), 6–17.

Cristofaro, M. (2022). 'Organizational sensemaking: A systematic review and a co-evolutionary model'. *European Management Journal*, **40**(3), 393–405.

Cristofaro, M., Abatecola, G., Giannetti, F. and Zannoni, A. (2024). 'The survival of the fastest: Unveiling the determinants of unicorns and gazelles' early success'. *Scandinavian Journal of Management*, **40**(2), 101335.

Cristofaro, M., Abatecola, G. and Kask, J. (2024). 'Business network paradoxes: A literature review and co-evolutionary perspective'. *Industrial Marketing Management*, **120**, 115–131.

Cristofaro, M., Augier, M., Lovallo, D., Abatecola, G. and Leoni, L. (2024). 'Behavioral strategy in evolution: A review and conceptual framework'. *European Management Journal*, https://doi.org/10.1016/j.emj.2024.10.002.

Cucari, N., Esposito De Falco, S., Yamak, S. and Lee, B. (Eds., 2023). *Handbook of research methods for corporate governance*. Edward Elgar.

Cyert, R.M. and March, J.G. (1963). *A behavioural theory of the firm*. Prentice-Hall.

Darwin, C.R. (1859). *On the origin of species by means of natural selection or the preservation of favoured races in the struggle for life*. John Murray.

D'Aveni, R.A. (1989). 'The aftermath of organizational decline: A longitudinal study of the strategic and managerial characteristics of declining firms'. *Academy of Management Journal*, **32**(3), 577–605.

D'Aveni, R.A. (1994). *Hypercompetition. Managing the dynamics of strategic maneuvering*. Free Press.

D'Aveni, R.A. and MacMillan, I.C. (1990). 'Crisis and the content of managerial communications: A study of the focus of attention of top managers in surviving and failing firms'. *Administrative Science Quarterly*, **35**(4), 634–657.

David, P.A. (1985). 'Clio and the economics of QWERTY'. *American Economic Review*, **75**(2), 332–337.

Davies, G., Chun, R., da Silva, R. and Roper, S. (2003). *Corporate reputation and competitiveness*. Routledge.

Dawkins, R. (1976). *The selfish gene*. Oxford University Press.

De Bono, E. (1970). *Lateral thinking. A textbook of creativity*. Penguin Books.

Delbufalo, E. (2012). 'Outcomes of inter-organizational trust in supply chain relationships: A systematic literature review and a meta-analysis of the empirical evidence'. *Supply Chain Management: An International Journal*, **17**(4), 377–402.

De Ruysscher, D. (2017). 'Business rescue, turnaround management, and the legal regime of default and insolvency in Western history (late middle ages to present day)'. In J. Adriaanse and J.P. van der Rest (Eds.), *Turnaround management and bankruptcy*. Routledge, 22–42.

Dess, G.G. and Beard, D.W. (1984). 'Dimensions of organizational task environments'. *Administrative Science Quarterly*, **29**(1), 52–73.

De Vita, L., Mari, M. and Poggesi, S. (2014). 'Women entrepreneurs in and from developing countries: Evidences from the literature'. *European Management Journal*, **32**(3), 451–460.

Dew, N. and Sarasvathy, S.D. (2016). 'Exaptation and niche construction: Behavioral insights for an evolutionary theory'. *Industrial and Corporate Change*, **25**(1), 167–179.

Dewaelheyns, N., De Prijcker, S. and Van Den Heuvel, K. (2017). 'Predicting business failure'. In J. Adriaanse and J.P. van der Rest (Eds.), *Turnaround management and bankruptcy*. Routledge, 66–45.

Di Maggio, P.J. and Powell, W.W. (1983). 'The iron cage revisited: Institutional isomorphism and collective rationality in organizational fields'. *American Sociological Review*, **48**(2), 147–160.

Di Minin, A., Frattini, F. and Piccaluga, A. (2010). 'Fiat: Open innovation in a downturn (1993–2003)'. *California Management Review*, **52**(3), 132–159.

Dimov, D. (2017). *The reflective entrepreneur*. Routledge.

Dobson, S., Jones, P., Agyapong, D. and Maas, G. (Eds., 2021). *Enterprising Africa: Transformation through entrepreneurship*. Routledge.

Donaldson, G. (1994). *Corporate restructuring. Managing the process from within*. Harvard Business School Press.

Dosi, G. (1982). 'Technological paradigms and technological trajectories: A suggested interpretation of the determinants and directions of technical change'. *Research Policy*, **11**(3), 147–162.

Dosi, G. (2023). *The foundation of complex evolving economics. Part one: Innovation, organization, and industrial dynamics*. Oxford University Press.

Dowell, G.W.S., Shackell, M.B. and Stuart, N.V. (2011). 'Boards, CEOs, and surviving a crisis: Evidence from the Internet shakeout'. *Strategic Management Journal*, **32**(10), 1025–1045.

Durand, R. (2006). *Organizational evolution and strategic management*. Sage.

Eldredge, N. and Gould, S.J. (1972). 'Punctuated equilibria: An alternative to phyletic gradualism'. In T.J.M. Schopf (Ed.), *Models in paleobiology*. Freeman, Cooper, 82-115.

Eldredge, N., Pievani, T., Serrelli, E. and Temkin, I. (Eds., 2016). *Evolutionary theory. A hierarchical perspective*. Chicago University Press.

Emery, F.E. and Trist, E.L. (1965). 'The causal texture of organizational environments'. *Human Relations*, **18**(1), 21–32.
England, P. and Farkas, G. (1986). *Households, employment and gender*. Aldine.
Enron Corporation (2000). *Annual report*.
Feldman, M.S. and Pentland, B.T. (2003). 'Reconceptualizing organizational routines as a source of flexibility and change'. *Administrative Science Quarterly*, **48**(1), 94–118.
Felin, T., Kauffman, S., Koppl, R. and Longo, G. (2014). 'Economic opportunity and evolution: Beyond landscapes and bounded rationality'. *Strategic Entrepreneurship Journal*, **8**(4), 269–282.
Fichman, M. and Levinthal, D.A. (1991). 'Honeymoons and the liability of adolescence: A new perspective on duration dependence in social and organizational relationships'. *Academy of Management Review*, **16**(2), 442–468.
Fleck, J. (2000). 'Artefact ↔ activity: The co-evolution of artefacts, knowledge and organization in technological innovation'. In J. Ziman (Ed.), *Technological innovation as an evolutionary process*. Cambridge University Press, 248–266.
Fortune, A. and Mitchell, W. (2012). 'Unpacking firm exit at the firm and industry levels: The adaptation and selection of firm capabilities'. *Strategic Management Journal*, **33**(7), 794–819.
Foss, N.J. (2021). 'The impact of the Covid-19 pandemic on firm's organizational designs'. *Journal of Management Studies*, **58**(1), 270–274.
Freeman, J., Carroll, G.R. and Hannan, M.T. (1983). 'The liability of newness: Age dependence in organizational death rates'. *American Sociological Review*, **48**(5), 692–710.
Fruhan, W.E. (1979). *Financial strategy: Studies in the creation, transfer and destruction of shareholder value*. Irwin.
Galbraith, J.K. (1987). *Economics in perspective: A critical history*. Princeton University Press.
Gallucci, C., Santulli, R., Modina, M. and Formisano, V. (2023). 'Financial ratios, corporate governance and bank-firm information: A Bayesian approach to predict SMEs' default'. *Journal of Management and Governance*, **27**(3), 873–892.
Gambardella, A., Panico, C. and Valentini, G. (2015). 'Strategic incentives to human capital'. *Strategic Management Journal*, **36**(1), 37–52.
Garud, R., Gehman, J. and Giuliani, A.P. (2016). 'Technological exaptation: A narrative approach'. *Industrial and Corporate Change*, **25**(1), 149–166.
Gatti, C., Volpe, L. and Vagnani, G. (2015). 'Interdependence among productive activities: Implications for exploration and exploitation'. *Journal of Business Research*, **68**(3), 711–722.
Giardino, P., Delladio, S., Baiocco, S. and Caputo, A. (2023). 'Beyond myth: A systematic literature review on the emergence of unicorn firms'. *Journal of Small Business and Enterprise Development*, **30**(6), 1156–1177.
Gill, J. and Price, I. (2022). 'A meme-based research programme for management and organization studies'. *International Journal of Management Reviews*, **24**(3), 415–432.
Gimenez-Fernandez, E.M., Sandulli, F.D. and Bogers, M. (2020). 'Unpacking liabilities of newness and smallness in innovative start-ups: Investigating the differences in innovation performance between new and older small firms'. *Research Policy*, **49**(10), 104049.

Gnan, L., Hinna, A., Monteduro, F. and Scarozza, D. (2013). 'Corporate governance and management practices: Stakeholder involvement, quality and sustainability tools adoption: Evidences in local public utilities'. *Journal of Management and Governance*, **17**(4), 907–937.

Golinelli, G.M. (2010). *Viable Systems Approach (VSA). Governing business dynamics*. CEDAM.

Gordini, N. (2014). 'A genetic algorithm approach for SME bankruptcy prediction: Empirical evidence from Italy'. *Expert Systems with Applications*, **41**(14), 6433–6445.

Gould, S.J. and Vrba, E.S. (1982). 'Exaptation. A missing term in the science of form'. *Paleobiology*, **8**(3), 4–15.

Gowdy, J.E., Dollimore, D.E., Wilson, D.S. and Witt, U. (2013). 'Economic cosmology and the evolutionary challenge'. *Journal of Economic Behaviour and Organization*, **90**, S11–S20.

Grandinetti, R. (2018). 'Is organizational evolution Darwinian and/or Lamarckian?'. *International Journal of Organizational Analysis*, **26**(5), 858–874.

Grant, R.M. (2024). *Contemporary strategy analysis* (12th edition). John Wiley & Sons.

Greve, H.R., Palmer, D. and Pozner, J.-E. (2010). 'Organizations gone wild: The causes, processes, and consequences of organizational misconduct'. *Academy of Management Annals*, **4**(1), 53–107.

Grodal, S., Gotsopoulos, A. and Suarez, F. (2015). 'The co-evolution of technologies and categories during industry emergence'. *Academy of Management Review*, **40**(3), 420–445.

Guatri, L. (1995). *Turnaround. Declino, crisi e ritorno al valore*. EGEA.

Gudmundsson, S.V. and Lechner, C. (2013). 'Cognitive biases, organization, and entrepreneurial firm survival'. *European Management Journal*, **31**(3), 278–294.

Guercini, S. and Milanesi, M. (2016). 'Interaction approach and liabilities: A case analysis of start-up firms'. *Journal of Business-to-Business Marketing*, **23**(4), 293–309.

Gundel, S. (2005). 'Towards a new typology of crises'. *Journal of Contingencies and Crisis Management*, **13**(3), 106–115.

Hall, D.J. and Saias, M.A. (1980). 'Strategy follows structure!'. *Strategic Management Journal*, **1**(2), 149–163.

Hambrick, D.C. and D'Aveni, R.A. (1988). 'Large corporate failures as downward spirals'. *Administrative Science Quarterly*, **33**(1), 1–23.

Hambrick, D.C. and D'Aveni, R.A. (1992). 'Top team deterioration as part of the downward spiral of large corporate bankruptcies'. *Management Science*, **38**(10), 1445–1466.

Hambrick, D.C. and Mason, P.A. (1984). 'Upper echelons: The organization as a reflection of its top managers'. *Academy of Management Review*, **9**(2), 193–206.

Hammond, J.S. III, Keeney, R.L. and Raiffa, H. (1998). 'The hidden traps of decision making'. *Harvard Business Review*, **76**(5), 47–58.

Han, J.-H., Pollock, T.G and Graffin, S.D. (2024). 'Now you see me: How status and categorical proximity shape misconduct scandalization'. *Academy of Management Journal*, **67**(1), 208–231.

Hannan, M.T. and Freeman, J.H. (1977). 'The population ecology of organizations'. *American Journal of Sociology*, **82**(5), 929–964.

Hannan, M.T. and Freeman, J.H. (1984). 'Structural inertia and organizational change'. *American Sociological Review*, **49**(2), 149–164.

Harrison, S.H. Hua, M. and Deasy, D. (2024). '*Scar tissue that I wish you saw*: Creativity scars and their impact on creative work'. *Academy of Management Discoveries*, https://doi.org/10.5465/amd.2023.0141.

Hegel, G.W.F. (1807). *Phänomenologie des Geistes.*

Henderson, A.D. (1999). 'Firm strategy and age dependence: A contingent view of the liabilities of newness, adolescence and obsolescence'. *Administrative Science Quarterly*, **44**(2), 281–314.

Hmieleski, K.M. and Baron, R.A. (2009). 'Entrepreneurs' optimism and new venture performance: A social cognitive perspective'. *Academy of Management Journal*, **52**(3), 473–488.

Hodgson, G.M. and Knudsen, T. (2010). *Darwin's conjecture: The search for general principles of social and economic evolution.* University of Chicago Press.

Hrebiniak, L.G. and Joyce, W.F. (1984). *Implementing strategy.* MacMillan.

Hrebiniak, L.G. and Joyce, W.F. (1985). 'Organizational adaptation: Strategic choice and environmental determinism'. *Administrative Science Quarterly*, **30**(3), 336–349.

Hristov, I., Camilli, R., Chirico, A. and Mechelli, A. (2024). 'The integration between enterprise risk management and performance management system: Managerial analysis and conceptual model to support strategic decision-making process'. *Production Planning and Control*, **35**(8), 842–855.

Hull, D.L. (1988). *Science as a process.* University of Chicago Press.

Huxley, J. (1942). *Evolution: The modern synthesis.* Harper & Brothers.

Iandolo, F., La Sala, A., Turriziani, L. and Caputo, F. (2024). 'Stakeholder engagement in managing systemic risk management'. *Business Ethics, the Environment & Responsibility*, https://doi.org/10.1111/beer.12694.

International Organization for Migration (2017). *Migration in the 2030 agenda.* Retrieved from https://www.iom.int/sites/default/files/about-iom/gender/Migration-in-the-2030-Agenda-SDGs-Achieving-Gender-Equality-through-Migration-Governance.pdf (Last access: November 6, 2024).

Jacobides, M.G. and Winter, S.G. (2005). 'The co-evolution of capabilities and transaction costs: Explaining the institutional structure of production'. *Strategic Management Journal*, **26**(5), 395–413.

Janis, I.L. (1972). *Victims of groupthink: A psychological study of foreign-policy decisions and fiascoes.* Houghton Mifflin.

Janzen, D. (1980). 'When is it coevolution?'. *Evolution*, **34**(3), 611–612.

Jennings, J.E. and Brush, C.G. (2013). 'Research on women entrepreneurs: Challenges to (and from) the broader entrepreneurship literature?'. *Academy of Management Annals*, **7**(1), 663–715.

Jiang, G.H., Kotabe, M., Hamilton, R.D. and Smith, S.W. (2016). 'Early internationalization and the role of immigration in new venture survival'. *International Business Review*, **25**(6), 1285–1296.

Johanson, J. and Vahlne, J.E. (2009). 'The Uppsala internationalization process model revisited: From liability of foreignness to liability of outsidership'. *Journal of International Business Studies*, **40**, 1411–1431.

Johansson, T. and Kask, J. (2013). 'On the promise and premises of a Darwinian theory in research on business relationships'. *Industrial Marketing Management*, **42**(3), 306–315.

Jones, C. and Walter, G. (2017). *An autecological theory of the firm and its environment.* Edward Elgar.

Josefy, M.A., Harrison, J.S., Sirmon, D.G. and Carnes, C. (2017). 'Living and dying: Synthesizing the literature on firm survival and failure across stages of development'. *Academy of Management Annals*, **11**(2), 770–799.

Kaplan, R.S. and Mikes, A. (2012). 'Managing risks: A new framework'. *Harvard Business Review*, **90**(6), 48–60.

Kask, J. and Linton, G. (2023). 'Editorial: Five principles for overcoming obstacles in deep-tech startup journeys'. *Journal of Small Business and Enterprise Development*, **30**(1), 1–3.

Konig, A.S., Graf-Vlachy, L., Bundy, J.N. and Little, L. (2020). 'A blessing and a curse: How CEOs' empathy affects their management of organizational crises'. *Academy of Management Review*, **45**(1), 130–153.

Laland, K., Uller, T., Feldman, M., Sterelny, K., Muller, G.B., Moczek, A., Jablonka, E., Odling-Smee, J., Wray, G.A., Hoekstra, H.E., Futuyma, D.J., Lenski, R.E., Mackay, T.F.C., Schluter, D. and Strassmann, J.E. (2014). 'Does evolutionary theory need a rethink?' *Nature*, **514**, 161–164.

La Rocca, A., Perna, A., Snehota, I. and Ciabuschi, F. (2019). 'The role of supplier relationships in the development of new business ventures'. *Industrial Marketing Management*, **80**, 149–159.

Lawless, M.W. and Finch, L.K. (1989). 'Choice and determinism: A test of Hrebiniak and Joyce's framework on strategy-environment fit'. *Strategic Management Journal*, **10**(4), 351–365.

Lawrence, P.R. and Lorsch, J.W. (1967). *Organization and environment: Managing differentiation and integration*. Harvard Business School Press.

Lee, A. (2013). *Welcome to the Unicorn club: Learning from billion-dollar start-ups*. Retrieved from https://techcrunch.com/2013/11/02/welcome-to-the-unicorn-club/ (Last access: November 4, 2024).

Lee, M. and Huang, L. (2018). 'Gender bias, social impact framing, and evaluation of entrepreneurial ventures'. *Organization Science*, **29**(1), 1–16.

Lee, S.H., Yamakawa, Y., Peng, M.V. and Barney, J.B. (2011). 'How do bankruptcy laws affect entrepreneurship development around the world?'. *Journal of Business Venturing*, **26**(5), 505–520.

Leoni, L. and Cristofaro, M. (2022). 'To adopt or not to adopt? A co-evolutionary framework and paradox of technology adoption by small museums'. *Current Issues in Tourism*, **25**(18), 2969–2990.

Levinthal, D.A. (2021). *Evolutionary processes and organizational adaptation: A Mendelian perspective on strategic management*. Oxford University Press.

Levinthal, D.A. and Fichman, M. (1988). 'Dynamics of interorganizational attachments: Auditor-client relationships'. *Administrative Science Quarterly*, **33(**3), 345–506.

Levinthal, D.A. and Pham, D.N. (2024). 'Bringing politics back in: The role of power and coalitions in organizational adaptation'. *Organization Science*, **35**(5), 1704–1720.

Levitt, T. (1965). 'Exploit the product life cycle'. *Harvard Business Review*, **43**(6), 81–94.

Lewin, A.Y. and Volberda, H.K. (1999). 'Prolegomena on co-evolution: A framework for research on strategy and new organizational forms'. *Organization Science*, **10**(5), 519–534.

Lewontin, R.C. (1978). 'Adaptation'. *Scientific American*, **239**(3), 212–28.

Lewontin, R.C. (1983). 'The organism as the subject and object of evolution'. *Scientia*, **118**, 63–82.

Lloyd, E.A. and Gould, S.J. (2017). 'Exaptation revisited: Changes imposed by evolutionary psychologists and behavioral biologists'. *Biological Theory*, **12**(1), 50–65.

Lohrke, F.T., Bedeian, A.G. and Palmer, T.B. (2004). 'The role of top management teams in formulating and implementing turnaround strategies: A review and research agenda'. *International Journal of Management Reviews*, **5-6**(2), 63–90.

Lombardi, R., Trequattrini, R. and Russo, G. (2016). 'Innovative start-ups and equity crowd-funding'. *International Journal of Risk Assessment and Management*, **19**(1-2), 68–83.

Lounsbury, M. and Ventresca, M.J. (Eds., 2002). *Research in the sociology of organizations, vol 19: Social structure and organizations revisited.* Elsevier.

Lovallo, D., Cristofaro, M. and Flyvbjerg, B. (2023). 'Governing large projects: A three- stage process to get it right'. *Academy of Management Perspectives*, **37**(2), 138–156.

Malerba, F. and Lee, K. (2017). 'An evolutionary perspective on economic catch-up by latecomers'. *Industrial and Corporate Change*, **30**(4), 986–1010.

Malki, B., Uman, T. and Pittino, D. (2020). 'The entrepreneurial financing of the immigrant entrepreneurs: A literature review'. *Small Business Economics*, **58**(3), 1337–1365.

Manesh, M.F., Flamini, G., Petrolo, D. and Palumbo, R. (2022). 'A round of dancing and then one more: Embedding intuition in the ballet of entrepreneurial decision making'. *International Entrepreneurship and Management Journal*, **18**(2), 499–528.

Marengo, L., Settepanella, S. and Valente, M. (2023). 'Mendelian explorations'. *Journal of Organization Design*, **12**, 157–163.

Mari, M. and Poggesi, S. (2024). *Current trends in female entrepreneurship: Innovation and immigration*. Emerald.

Mari, M., Poggesi, S., Abatecola, G. and Essers, C. (2024). 'Women entrepreneurs and innovation: Retrospect and prospect'. *Journal of Innovation & Knowledge*, **9**(3), 100519.

Marquis, C. and Huang, Z. (2010). 'Acquisitions as exaptation: The legacy of founding institutions in the US commercial banking industry'. *Academy of Management Journal*, **53**(6), 1141–1473.

Marquis, C. and Tilcsik, A. (2013). 'Imprinting: Toward a multilevel theory'. *Academy of Management Annals*, **7**(1), 193–243.

Mata, J. and Alves, C. (2018). 'The survival of firms founded by immigrants: Institutional distance between home and host country, and experience in the host country'. *Strategic Management Journal*, **39**(11), 2965–2991.

Mata, J. and Portugal, P. (2002). 'The survival of new domestic and foreign-owned firms'. *Strategic Management Journal*, **23**(4), 323–343.

Mazzucato, M. (2018). *The value of everything. Making and taking in the global economy*. Penguin Books.

McCarthy, I.P., Collard, M. and Johnson, M. (2017). 'Adaptive organizational resilience: An evolutionary perspective'. *Current Opinion in Environmental Sustainability*, **28**, 33–40.

McCarthy, I.P., Lawrence, T.B., Wixted, B. and Gordon, B. (2010). 'A multidimensional conceptualization of environmental velocity'. *Academy of Management Review*, **35**(4), 604–626.

McKelvey, B. (1997). 'Quasi-natural organization science'. *Organization Science*, **8**(4), 352–380.

McKinley, W., Latham, S. and Braun, M. (2014). 'Organizational decline and innovation: Turnarounds and downward spirals'. *Academy of Management Review*, **39**(1), 88–110.

McLean, B. (2001). 'Is Enron Overpriced?'. *Fortune*, March 5.

Mechelli, A. and Cimini, R. (2021). 'The effect of corporate governance and investor protection environments on the value relevance of new accounting standards: The case of IFRS 9 and IAS 39'. *Journal of Management and Governance*, **25**(4), 1241–1266.

Mellahi, K., Jackson, P. and Sparks, L. (2002). 'An exploratory study into failure in successful organizations: The case of Marks & Spencer'. *British Journal of Management*, **13**(1), 15–29.

Mellahi, K. and Wilkinson, A. (2004). 'Organizational failure: A critique of recent research and a proposed integrative framework'. *International Journal of Management Reviews*, **5-6**(1), 21–41.

Meyer, M.W. (1990). 'Notes of a skeptic: From organizational ecology to organizational evolution'. In J.V. Singh (Ed.), *Organizational evolution: New directions*. Sage, 298–314.

Micelotta, E., Washington, M. and Docekalova, I. (2018). 'Industry gender imprinting and new venture creation: The liabilities of women's leagues in the sports industry'. *Entrepreneurship Theory and Practice*, **42**(1), 94–128.

Milburn, T.W., Schuler, R.S. and Watman, K.H. (1983). 'Organizational crisis. Part I: Definition and conceptualization'. *Human Relations*, **36**(12), 1161–1180.

Miller, D. (1986). 'Configurations of strategy and structure: Towards a synthesis'. *Strategic Management Journal*, **7**(3), 233–249.

Miller, D. (1990). *The Icarus paradox: How exceptional companies bring about their own downfall. New lessons in the dynamics of corporate success, decline, and renewal.* Harper Business.

Milne, A. (1961). 'Definition of competition among animals'. In F.L. Milnethorpe (Ed.), *Mechanisms in biological competition*. Cambridge University Press, 40–61.

Mindes, S.C.H. and Lewin, P. (2023). 'Intersectional dimensions of entrepreneurship among immigrant Hispanic women'. *Journal of Small Business Management*, **62**(5), 2181–2210.

Minichilli, A. and Hansen, C. (2007). 'The board advisory tasks in small firms and the event of crises'. *Journal of Management and Governance*, **11**(1), 5–22.

Mintzberg, H. (1990). 'The Design School: Reconsidering the basic premises of strategic management'. *Strategic Management Journal*, **11**(3), 171–195.

Miralles, M., Lee, B., Dörfler, V. and Stierand, M. (2022). 'Guest editorial: Investigating trauma: Methodological, emotional and ethical challenges for the qualitative researcher'. *Qualitative Research in Organizations and Management*, **17**(4), 397–405.

Mitroff, I.I. (1988). 'Crisis management: Cutting through the confusion'. *Sloan Management Review*, **29**(2), 15–20.

Mitroff, I.I. and Pearson, C.M. (1993). *Crisis management. Diagnostic guide for improving your organization crisis-preparedness*. Jossey-Bass.

Mollick, E. (2020). *The Unicorn's shadow: Combating the dangerous myths that hold back startups, founders, and investors*. Wharton School Press.

Morrow, J.L., Sirmon, D.G., Hitt, M.A. and Holcomb, T.R. (2007). 'Creating value in the face of declining performance: Firm strategies and organizational recovery'. *Strategic Management Journal*, **28**(3), 271–283.

Murmann, J.P. (2003). *Knowledge and competitive advantage: The co-evolution of firms, technology and national institutions*. Cambridge University Press.

Murmann, J.P. (2013). 'The co-evolution of industries and important features of their environments'. *Organization Science*, **24**(1), 58–78.

Murphy, P.J. (2011).'A 2x2 conceptual foundation for entrepreneurial discovery theory'. *Entrepreneurship Theory and Practice*, **35**(2), 359–374.

Murphy, P.J. (2022). 'Editorial: Passion: An entrepreneurial constant'. *Journal of Small Business and Enterprise Development*, **29**(7), 993–993.

Ndofor, H.A., Vanevenhoven, J. and Barker, V.L. (2013). 'Software firm turnarounds in the 1990s: An analysis of reversing decline in a growing, dynamic industry'. *Strategic Management Journal*, **34**(9), 1123–1133.

Nelson, R.R. and Winter, S.G. (1982). *An evolutionary theory of economic change*. Harvard University Press.

Nuismer, S.L. (2017). *Introduction to coevolutionary theory*. W.H. Freeman.

Osborn, H.F. (1905). 'Tyrannosaurus and other Cretaceous carnivorous dinosaurs'. *Bulletin of the American Museum of Natural History*, **21**, 259–265.

Paesano, A. and Risso, M. (2024). 'A synergy of spirituality and technologies toward a society 5.0'. In M. Del Baldo, M.G. Baldarelli and E. Righini (Eds.), *Place based approaches to sustainability volume II. Business, economics, and social models*. Palgrave Macmillan, 143–175.

Paniccia, P.M.A., Abatecola, G. and Baiocco, S. (2024). 'Integrating time and knowledge to understand organizational evolution: Towards a conceptual framework'. *Journal of Knowledge Management*, **18**(11), 62–77.

Paniccia, P.M.A. and Baiocco, S. (2021). 'Interpreting sustainable agritourism through co-evolution of social organizations'. *Journal of Sustainable Tourism*, **29**(1), 87–105.

Paniccia, P.M.A. and Leoni, L. (2019). 'Co-evolution in tourism: The case of albergo diffuso'. *Current Issues in Tourism*, **22**(10), 1216–1243.

Papa, A., Dezi, L., Gregori, G.L., Mueller, J. and Miglietta, N. (2020). 'Improving innovation performance through knowledge acquisition: The moderating role of employee retention and human resource management practices'. *Journal of Knowledge Management*, **24**(3), 589–605.

Parks, G.M. (1977). 'How to climb a growth curve: Eleven hurdles for the entrepreneur-manager'. *Journal of Small Business Management*, **15**(1), 25–29, and **15**(2), 45–49.

Pauchant, T.C. and Mitroff, I.I. (1992). *Transforming the crisis-prone organization. Preventing individual, organizational and environmental tragedies*. Jossey-Bass.

Pearson, C. and Clair, J. (1998). 'Reframing crisis management'. *Academy of Management Review*, **23**(1), 59–76.

Penrose, E.T. (1959). *The theory of the growth of the firm*. Oxford University Press.

Pentland, B.T., Feldman, M.S., Becker, M.C. and Liu, P. (2012). 'Dynamics of organizational routines: A generative model'. *Journal of Management Studies*, **49**(8), 1484–1508.

Pereira, V., Corradini, C., Temouri, Y. and Mellahi, K. (2020). 'Investigating institutional, economic and social determinants of European regions for firm growth through employment generation'. *British Journal of Management*, **31**(1), 162–183.

Pettigrew, A.M. (1979). 'On studying organizational cultures'. *Administrative Science Quarterly*, **24**(4), 570–581.

Pettigrew, A.M. (1987). 'Context and action in the transformation of the firm'. *Journal of Management Studies*, **24**(6), 649–670.

Pham, D., Jones, P., Dobson, S., Linan, F. and Viala, C. (2021). 'Entrepreneurial implementation intention as a tool to moderate the stability of entrepreneurial goal intention: A sensemaking approach'. *Journal of Business Research*, **123**, 97–105.

Phelps, R., Adams, R. and Bessant, J. (2007). 'Life cycles of growing organizations: A review with implications for knowledge and learning'. *International Journal of Management Reviews*, **9**(1), 1–30.

Picone, P.M., Dagnino, G.B. and Minà, A. (2014). 'The origin of failure: A multidimensional appraisal of the hubris hypothesis and proposed research agenda'. *Academy of Management Perspectives*, **28**(4), 447–468.

Pigliucci, M. and Müller, G.B. (Eds., 2010). *Evolution, the extended synthesis*. MIT Press.

Porter, M.E. (1985). *Competitive advantage. Creating and sustaining superior performance*. Free Press.

Powell, T.C., Lovallo, D. and Fox, C.R. (2011). 'Behavioral strategy'. *Strategic Management Journal*, **32**(13), 1369–1386.

Rajan, R.G. and Zingales, L. (2004). *Saving capitalism from the capitalists. Unleashing the power of financial markets to create wealth and spread opportunity*. Princeton University Press.

Randolph-Seng, B. (2009). 'The (mis)management of agency: Conscious belief and nonconscious self-control'. *Behavioral and Brain Sciences*, **32**(6), 532–533.

Rappaport, A. (1986). *Creating shareholder value. The new standard for business performance*. Free Press.

Reydon, T.A.C. and Scholz, M. (2009). 'Why organizational ecology is not a Darwinian research program'. *Philosophy of the Social Sciences*, **39**(3), 408–439.

Ricciotti, F., Cristofaro, M., Abatecola, G. and Mari, M. (2022). 'Executive profiles and performance of real estate services: Evidence of *reverse causality* from Europe'. *Cities*, **130**, 103854.

Ritala, P. and Almpanopoulou, A. (2017). 'In defense of "eco" in innovation ecosystem'. *Techovation*, **60-61**, 39–42.

Rizzi, F. and Frey, M. (2014). 'Sustainable co-evolution of environmental regulation and oligopolies: Moving towards a managerial theory of meta-organisational approaches'. *International Journal of Innovation and Sustainable Development*, **8**(3), 270–289.

Roberto, M.A. (2019). *Unlocking creativity: How to solve any problem and make the best decisions by shifting creative mindsets*. John Wiley & Sons.

Rogers, W. et al. (1986). *Report of the Presidential Commission on the space shuttle Challenger accident*. Washington DC.

Romanelli, E. and Tushman, M.L. (1994). 'Organizational transformation as punctuated equilibrium: An empirical test'. *Academy of Management Journal*, **37**(5), 1141–1166.

Rosenberg, S. (1987). 'Psst, Los Angeles has already won the title'. *Los Angeles Times*, May 30, 12.

Sadun, R., Fuller, J.B., Hansen, S. and Neal, PJ. 'The C-Suite skills that matter most'. *Harvard Business Review*, **100**(4), 42–50.

Sandberg, S. and Grant, A. (2017). *Option B. Facing adversity, building resilience, and finding joy*. Penguin Random House.

Sandhu, S. and Kulik, C. (2019). 'Shaping and being shaped: How organizational structure and managerial discretion co-evolve in new managerial roles'. *Administrative Science Quarterly*, **64**(3), 619–658.

Santangelo, G.D. and Stucchi, T. (2018). 'Internationalization through exaptation: The role of domestic geographical dispersion in the internationalization process'. *Journal of International Business Studies*, **49**(6), 753–760.

Sarta, A., Durand, R. and Vergne, J.-P. (2021). 'Organizational adaptation'. *Journal of Management*, **47**(1), 43–75.

Saviano, M., Nenci, L. and Caputo, F. (2017). 'The financial gap for women in the MENA region: A systemic perspective'. *Gender in Management*, **32**(3), 203–217.

Scafarto, F., Poggesi, S. and Mari, M. (2019). 'Entrepreneurial intentions, risk-taking propensity and environmental support: The Italian experience'. In A. Caputo and M.M. Pellegrini (Eds.), *The anatomy of entrepreneurial decisions. Past, present and future research directions*. Springer, 218–231.

Schiavone, F., Zeuli, F., Perillo, C. and Bastone, A. (2024). 'Enhancing sense-making through intellectual capital: Evidence from a healthcare network'. *Journal of Innovation & Knowledge*, **9**(4), 100619.

Schlaile, M. (Ed., 2021). *Memetics and evolutionary economics. To boldly go where no meme has gone before*. Springer.

Schmitt, A., Barker, V.L., Raisch, S. and Whetten, D. (2016). 'Strategic renewal in times of environmental scarcity'. *Long Range Planning*, **49**(3), 361–376.

Schmitt, A. and Raisch, S. (2013). 'Corporate turnarounds: The duality of retrenchment and recovery'. *Journal of Management Studies*, **50**(7), 1216–1244.

Scuotto, V., Garcia-Perez, A., Cillo, V. and Giacosa, E. (2020). 'Do stakeholder capabilities promote sustainable business innovation in small and medium-sized enterprises? Evidence from Italy'. *Journal of Business Research*, **119**, 131–141.

Secchi, D. and Cowley, S.J. (2021). 'Cognition in organisations: What it is and how it works'. *European Management Review*, **18**(2), 79–92.

Shane, S. (2010). *Born entrepreneurs, born leaders. How your genes affect your work life*. Oxford University Press.

Shields, S.A. (2008). 'Gender: An intersectionality perspective'. *Sex Roles*, **59**, 301–311.

Shipp, A.J. and Jansen, K.J. (2021). 'The "other" time: A review of the subjective experience of time in organizations'. *Academy of Management Annals*, **15**(1), 299–334.

Shrivastava, P. (1992). *Bophal: Anatomy of a crisis* (2nd edition). Paul Chapman.

Shrivastava, P., Mitroff, I.I., Miller, D. and Miglani, A. (1988). 'Understanding industrial crises'. *Journal of Management Studies*, **25**(4), 285–303.

Siano, A., Vollero, A., Conte, F. and Amabile, S. (2017). '*More than words*: Expanding the taxonomy of greenwashing after the Volkswagen scandal'. *Journal of Business Research*, **71**, 27–37.

Simon, H.A. (1947). *Administrative behaviour. A study of decision-making processes in administrative organization*. Macmillan.

Simone, C., Barile, S. and Grandinetti, R. (2021). 'The emergence of new market spaces: Brokerage and firm cognitive endowment'. *Journal of Business Research*, **134**(4), 457–466.

Simsek, Z., Curtis Fox, B. and Heavey, C. (2015). 'What's past is prologue: A framework, re-view, and future directions for organizational research on imprinting'. *Journal of Management*, **41**(1), 288–317.

Singh, J.V., Tucker, D.J. and House, R.J. (1986). 'Organizational legitimacy and the liability of newness'. *Administrative Science Quarterly*, **31**(2), 171–193.

Slatter, S. (1984). *Corporate recovery: A guide to turnaround management*. Penguin Books.

Smart, C. and Vertinsky, I. (1977). 'Design for crisis decision units'. *Administrative Science Quarterly*, **22**(4), 640–657.

Soto-Simeone, A., Sirén, C. and Antretter, T. (2020). 'New venture survival: A review and extension'. *International Journal of Management Reviews*, **22**(4), 378–407.

Spisak, B., O'Brien, M., Nicholson, N. and van Vugt, M. (2015). 'Niche construction and the evolution of leadership'. *Academy of Management Review*, **40**(2), 291–306.

Stam, E. and Van de Ven, A.H. (2021). 'Entrepreneurial ecosystem elements'. *Small Business Economics*, **56**, 809–832.

Startupgenome (2024). *The global startup ecosystem report 2024*. Retrieved from https://startupgenome.com/reports/gser2024 (Last access: November 9, 2024).

Staw, B., Sandelands, L. and Dutton, J.E. (1981). 'Threat–rigidity cycles in organizational behavior: A multi-level analysis'. *Administrative Science Quarterly*, **26**(4), 501–524.

Stiglitz, N., Knudsen, T. and Becker, M.C. (2016). 'Adaptation and inertia in dynamic environments'. *Strategic Management Journal*, **37**(9), 1854–1864.

Stinchcombe, A.L. (1965). 'Social structure and organizations'. In J. March (Ed.), *Handbook of organizations*. Rand McNally, 142–193.

Stinchcombe, A.L. (2005). *The logic of social research*. University of Chicago Press.

Stoelhorst, J.W. (2008). 'The explanatory logic and ontological commitment of generalized Darwinism'. *Journal of Economic Methodology*, **15**(4), 343–363.

Stoelhorst, J.W. and Vishwanathan, P. (2024). 'A stakeholder theory of corporate governance'. *Academy of Management Review*, **49**(1), 107–134.

Surace, A. (2019). 'Complexity and leadership: The case of a military organization'. *International Journal of Organizational Analysis*, **27**(5), 1522–1541.

Sutton, R.I. (2010). *Good boss, bad boss. How to be the best ... and learn from the worst*. Business Plus.

Sydow, J. and Schreyögg, G. (Eds., 2013). *Self-reinforcing processes in and among organizations*. Palgrave Macmillan.

Sydow, J., Schreyögg, G. and Koch, J. (2009). 'Organizational path dependence: Opening the black box'. *Academy of Management Review*, **34**(4), 689–709.

Tangpong, C., Abebe, M. and Li, Z. (2015). 'A temporal approach to retrenchment and successful turnaround in declining firms'. *Journal of Management Studies*, **52**(5), 647–677.

Teece, D.J., Pisano, G. and Shuen, A. (1997). 'Dynamic capabilities and strategic management'. *Strategic Management Journal*, **18**(7), 509–533.

Thomas, L.D.W. and Ritala, P. (2022). 'Ecosystem legitimacy emergence. A collective action view'. *Journal of Management*, **48**(3), 515–541.

Thompson, J. (1982). *Interaction and coevolution*. University of Chicago Press.

Tippmann, E., Ambos, T.C., Del Giudice, M., Monaghan, S. and Ringov, D. (2023). 'Scale-ups and scaling in an international business context'. *Journal of World Business*, **58**(1), 101397.

Torchia, M., Calabrò, A. and Huse, M. (2011). 'Women directors on corporate boards: From Tokenism to critical mass'. *Journal of Business Ethics*, 102, 299–317.

Trahms, C.A., Achidi Ndofor, A. and Sirmon, D.G. (2013). 'Organizational decline and turnaround: A review and agenda for future research'. *Journal of Management*, **39**(5), 1277–1307.

Tripsas, M. and Gavetti, G. (2000). 'Capabilities, cognition and inertia: Evidence from digital imaging'. *Strategic Management Journal*, **21**(10/11), 1147–1161.

Troisi, R., Di Nauta, P. and Piciocchi, P. (2022). 'Private corruption: An integrated organizational model'. *European Management Review*, **19**(3), 476–486.

Uli, V. (2018). 'A multilevel co-evolutionary perspective on organizational adaptation. Evidence from the service industry'. *Business Process Management Journal*, **24**(3), 652–670.

US Bureau of Labor Statistics (2024). *Establishment age and survival data*. Retrieved from https://www.bls.gov/bdm/us_age_naics_00_table7.txt (Last access: November 4, 2024).

Van de Ven, A.H. and Poole, M.S. (1995). 'Explaining development and change in organizations'. *Academy of Management Review*, **20**(3), 510–541.

Van de Ven, A.H. and Poole, M.S. (2005). 'Alternative approaches for studying organizational change'. *Organization Studies*, **26**(9), 1377–1404.

Van den Bosch, F.A.J., Volberda, H.K. and de Boer, M. (1999). 'Co-evolution of firm absorptive capacity and knowledge environment: Organizational forms and combinative capabilities'. *Organization Science*, **10**(5), 551–568.

Van Witteeloostuijn, A. (1998). 'Bridging behavioral and economic theories of decline: Organizational inertia, strategic competition, and chronic failure'. *Management Science*, **44**(4), 501–518.

Vergne, J.-P. and Durand, R. (2010). 'The missing link between the theory and empirics of path dependence: Conceptual clarification, testability issue, and methodological implications'. *Journal of Management Studies*, **47**(4), 736–759.

Vergne, J.-P. and Durand, R. (2011). 'The path of most persistence: An evolutionary perspective on path dependence and dynamic capabilities'. *Organization Studies*, **32**(3), 365–382.

Volberda, H.K. and Lewin, A. (2003). 'Co-evolutionary dynamics within and between firms: From evolution to co-evolution'. *Journal of Management Studies*, **40**(8), 2111–2136.

Volpato, G. (2009). 'Fiat Group Automobiles - An Arabian phoenix in the international auto industry'. In M. Freyssenet (Ed.), *The second automobile revolution – Trajectories of the world carmakers in the 21st century*. Palgrave Macmillan, 287–308.

Weber, L. (2017). 'A sociocognitive view of repeated interfirm exchanges: How the co-evolution of trust and learning impacts subsequent contracts'. *Organization Science*, **28**(4), 744–759.

Weick, K.E. (1969). *The social psychology of organizing*. Addison-Wesley.

Weitzel, W. and Johnson, E. (1989). 'Decline in organizations: A literature integration and extension'. *Administrative Science Quarterly*, **34**(1), 91–109.

Whittington, R. (1988). 'Environmental structure and theories of strategic choice'. *Journal of Management Studies*, **25**(6), 521–536.

Wholey, D.R. and Brittain, J.W. (1986). 'Organizational ecology: Findings and implications'. *Academy of Management Review*, **11**(3), 513–533.

Wiesenfeld, B.M., Wurthmann, K. and Hambrick, D.C. (2008). 'The stigmatization and devaluation of elites associated with corporate failures – A process model'. *Academy of Management Review*, **33**(1), 231–251.

Wievel, W. and Hunter, A. (1985). 'The inter-organizational network as a resource: A comparative case study on organizational genesis'. *Administrative Science Quarterly*, **30**(4), 482–496.

Wood, G. and Wright, M. (2009). 'Private equity: A review and synthesis'. *International Journal of Management Reviews*, **11**(4), 361–380.

Yang, T. and Triana, M. (2019). 'Set up to fail: Explaining when women-led businesses are more likely to fail'. *Journal of Management*, **45**(3), 926–954.

Yu, H. (2018). *Leap. How to thrive in a world where everything can be copied.* PublicAffairs.

Zaheer, S. (1995). 'Overcoming the liability of foreignness'. *Academy of Management Journal*, **38**(2), 341–363.

Zahra, S.A, Sapienza, H.J. and Davidsson, P. (2006). 'Entrepreneurship and dynamic capabilities: A review, model and research agenda'. *Journal of Management Studies*, **43**(4), 917–955.

Zankl, J. and Grimes, M. (2024). 'Taming Unicorns: Toward a new normal of responsible entrepreneurship'. *Academy of Management Review*, **49**(4), 879–905.

Zannoni, A. (2024). 'Reviewing the gender gap in management and entrepreneurship: Environmental factors and co-evolutionary dynamics'. *International Journal of Globalisation and Small Business*, **14**(2), 138–167.

Zattoni, A. and Cuomo, F. (2008). 'Why adopt codes of good governance? A comparison of institutional and efficiency perspectives'. *Corporate Governance: An International Review*, **16**(1), 1–15.

Zollo, M. and Winter, S. (2002). 'Deliberate learning and the evolution of dynamic capabilities'. *Organization Science*, **13**(3), 339–351.

Index

Note: **Bold** page numbers refer to tables, *italic* page numbers refer to figures and page numbers followed by "n" refer to end notes.

For Product Safety Concerns and Information please contact our EU representative GPSR@taylorandfrancis.com Taylor & Francis Verlag GmbH, Kaufingerstraße 24, 80331 München, Germany

Printed and bound by CPI Group (UK) Ltd, Croydon, CR0 4YY
14/09/2026
02216256-0004